THE STU  NG

ONE WEEK LOAN

THE STUDENT GUIDE TO MOOTING

MICHAEL HAMMOND

Edited by Margaret Ross

DUNDEE UNIVERSITY PRESS
2010

First published in Great Britain in 2010 by
Dundee University Press
University of Dundee
Dundee DD1 4HN

www.dup.dundee.ac.uk

Copyright © Michael Hammond

ISBN 978 1 84586 113 1

No natural forests were destroyed to make this product;
only farmed timber was used and replanted.

British Library Cataloguing-in-Publication Data
A catalogue record for this book is available on request from the British Library

Typeset by Waverley Typesetters, Warham, Norfolk
Printed and bound by Bell & Bain Ltd, Glasgow

CONTENTS

FOREWORD

Everyone is daunted by their first appearance in court. Often it's not the legal argument which causes the most anxiety. Where do I sit? How do I address the judge? What is the correct way of citing authorities? These matters all loom large in the student's mind.

Taking part in a moot is a very useful experience. Participants learn the answers to these questions in a sympathetic environment. More importantly, they gain first-hand experience of the dynamics involved in litigation. They find out that the resolution of legal disputes is a vibrant and constructive process.

In *The Student Guide to Mooting* Michael Hammond provides lucid and practical advice. Everyone involved in this excellent activity will find it of great assistance.

LORD WOOLMAN
Judge of the Supreme Court
April 2010

PREFACE

Mooting as a part of legal education is developing and expanding in Scottish universities. The aim of this text is to act as an introduction for those new to the subject area while also providing a quick reference text for the more experienced competitor. This short book aims to raise the standard of legal argument made by Scottish law students undertaking internal, national and international mooting competitions. This book avoids using complex terminology to explain simple concepts. The two stage method in this text is designed to teach students not only how to moot but also how to make a structured and concise legal argument. The two stage method outlined in this text is supplemented by easy-to-understand examples, extended contents and index pages and helpful hints and tips. Appendix 1 provides a full example of the application of the two stage method to a real moot problem. The content is up to date as at 31 January 2010.

This book was written during my second year as an undergraduate law student at the University of Aberdeen. My thanks go to the staff at the law school there for their support and advice. I am grateful to Margaret Ross for her guidance and encouragement, and for editorial input. Thanks also go to the Aberdeen University Law Mooting Society committee for their support. Special thanks go to Brian and Joyce Hammond.

Chapter 1

INTRODUCTION TO MOOTING

What is a Moot?

A moot is a legal debate taking place in a mock court room setting. The **1.1** legal debate is based on a moot problem which consists of a mock factual situation containing a dispute about one or more points of law. Two legal teams, each consisting of two counsel working in partnership, devise and present an argument based on legal authority on behalf of their client. Each team argues the points of law with a view to convincing the judge that the case of their client should succeed. The judge of the moot weighs the arguments presented to him and passes judgment on the law and on the team winners of the moot. It is possible to lose on the law but, by presenting the more skilled and reasoned legal argument, win the moot. The clerk of the court assists the judge in procedural matters and ensures the smooth running of the moot. There is no jury, evidence is not given and the facts are not disputed in the moot, only the law is debated. The appellant is represented by counsel consisting of a junior counsel for the appellant and a senior counsel for the appellant. The respondent is represented by counsel consisting of a junior counsel for the respondent and a senior counsel for the respondent.

The Importance of Mooting

The ability to analyse legal problems from different angles and produce **1.2** dynamic solutions with the client's interest at heart is a skill that the legal profession demands from graduating law students. Mooting demands a high standard of legal analysis and the application of problem-solving skills sought by graduate employers.

In order to successfully compete in a mooting competition, students must develop legal analysis skills and hone the ability to produce a reasoned and structured legal argument while generating an accurate statement of the relevant law. Developing these skills early in legal education provides students with important skills for life that will be useful for law school, the legal profession and other contexts in which reasoned oral argument is required.

Taking part in mooting competitions also allows students to develop their confidence through making oral arguments and practising public speaking skills. Mooting combines legal research with practical skills to demonstrate to law students how a university legal education on paper is put into practice in the courts.

Mooting is a highly sociable activity and often mooting competitions are attended by members of the legal profession, legal practitioners and practising judges. Students can benefit by taking the opportunity to discuss, with practitioners and members of the legal profession, the skill of legal argument and their experiences of the legal profession.

The Layout of the Room

1.3   The judge sits at the head of the table opposite the lectern. The clerk is positioned to the judge's right. The appellants sit clerk side and the respondents sit to the judge's left. See the diagram below for layout.

Figure 1   The Layout of the Room

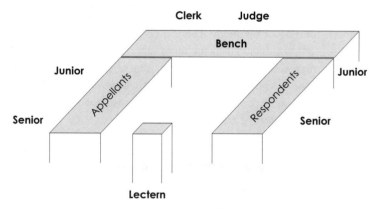

Chapter 2

COUNSEL

Introduction

This chapter addresses the procedure for counsel including: the order **2.1** of speech, counsel's ability to interrupt another counsel, and the role of junior and senior for each counsel including the basic requirements for each counsel's address to the court. These basic requirements form the skeleton of the legal argument that will be given by counsel. The skeleton structure of the argument is expanded upon in detail in Chapter 4.

Procedure for Counsel

Counsel speak in the following order: junior counsel for the appellant, **2.2** junior counsel for the respondent, senior counsel for the appellant and senior counsel for the respondent. Counsel presents argument within a set time period. The time constraint on counsel's presentation varies from competition to competition and generally senior counsel is entitled to longer than junior counsel.[1]

When counsel is speaking the opposing counsel are not entitled to make any objection or to interrupt in any way. Junior or senior counsel for the same side may pass notes to one another. The speaking counsel may ask the judge's permission to briefly discuss something with his partner* before returning to his speech or answering a question. Counsel must always stand when addressing the judge. At the beginning of the moot, senior counsel for the appellant introduces all other counsel to the judge.[2]

---

* Words importing the masculine gender include the feminine, unless the contrary is apparent.

[1] In Aberdeen University Law Mooting Society competitions junior counsel is entitled to ten minutes time and senior counsel is entitled to fifteen minutes.

[2] See para 7.6 below.

Brief Overview of the Role of Counsel

2.3 This section provides an introductory overview of the role of each counsel. Chapter 4 deals with the individual aspects of each counsel's role in substantive terms.

Junior counsel for the appellant

1. Introduces himself to the judge.
2. Offers to the judge a brief outline of the facts of the case at first instance.[3]
3. Puts the appeal question(s) to the court.
4. Outlines the submissions to be discussed by the appellants, indicating which of these will be dealt with by each counsel.
5. Provides the structure of his argument.
6. Deals with his submissions.
7. Concludes his submissions and argument.

Junior counsel for the respondent

1. Introduces himself to the judge.
2. May wish to draw the judge's attention to specific facts that are important to the argument of the respondents.
3. Makes any rebuttals of the arguments made by junior counsel for the respondents.
4. Puts the respondent's question(s) to the court.
5. Outlines the submissions to be discussed by the respondents, indicating which of these will be dealt with by each counsel.
6. Gives the structure of his argument.
7. Deals with his submissions.
8. Concludes his argument linking it back to the submissions.

Senior counsel for the appellant

1. Introduces himself to the judge.
2. May respond to the points made by the respondents, deals with any issues that have arisen concerning junior counsel for the appellant's submissions or argument.
3. Reminds the judge of the appellant's question to the court.
4. Outlines the submissions he will deal with.
5. Provides the structure of his argument.

---

[3] See para 7.7 below.

6. Deals with his submissions.
7. Concludes his argument linking it back to his submissions.
8. Concludes the arguments of the appellants in whole.[4]

Senior counsel for the respondent

1. Introduces himself to the judge.
2. May rebut points raised by the appellants.
3. Reminds the judge of the respondent's question to the court.
4. Outlines the submissions he will deal with.
5. Gives the structure of his argument.
6.. Deals with his submissions.
7. Concludes his argument linking it back to his submissions.
8. Concludes the argument of the respondents in whole.

Summary

This chapter has:

2.4

1. addressed the order of speech for counsel;
2. established that counsel cannot interrupt during the moot; and
3. formed the basic overview of the role of each counsel which will be expanded upon in Chapter 4.

---

[4] Unlike in English mooting competitions, counsel for the appellant has no right of reply after senior counsel for the respondent has concluded his argument.

Chapter 3

STAGE 1:
THE PROBLEM AND MOOT POINT

Introduction

Chapter 3 and Chapter 4 deal with a simple two stage method to address- **3.1**
ing a moot problem. Chapter 3 addresses the first approach to the moot
problem, whereas Chapter 4 deals with making the legal argument and
builds on the skeleton outline of the roles of counsel in Chapter 2. The first
approach to the moot problem involves looking at how to read the problem
page and identify the field of law, researching the basics and background
of the law, identifying the central moot points and discarding irrelevant
points and the allocation of different points of law, or lines of argument to
each counsel and the importance of team work. Figure 2 below outlines
the structure of stage 1 and provides references to the relevant sections of
Chapter 3 that deal with each part of stage 1.

Figure 2   Stage 1: The Problem and Moot Point

Stage 1: The problem and moot point	Reference
Read the problem and identify the field of law	para 3.2
Research	para 3.3
Identify the central moot points	para 3.4
Allocating points of law	para 3.5

Read the Problem and Identify the Field

The problem page contains a brief summary of the case at first instance **3.2**
including which court had heard the case, the facts of the case at first
instance, the decision in law of the court at first instance and, usually the
findings in fact of the court at first instance. Counsel's first task is to read

the problem over very carefully and identify the field of law involved. It may be criminal, delictual, contractual etc. Counsel should be aware that a complex problem may involve more than one field of law. Counsel should try to get a feel for the problem and how it might be possible to answer it. Counsel may find it useful to take notes of questions to research and draw diagrams or time lines of the facts of the case. Also, counsel should establish what side of the argument he is making and which client he represents. Having identified the field of law applicable it may be appropriate to do some background reading to confirm what the central issues of the case are and to rule out side issues.

Research

3.3 In general, the strength of a legal argument hinges on counsel's ability to research the field of law. If counsel's research is successful then authoritative law will be found which supports the case being made for his client.[5] Counsel should research principles that support his client's case and also principles that weaken it.[6] The first approach to research is background reading on the field of law concerned. There may be a central statute or case in the problem. Counsel must read the case and cases cited in it; look for commentaries on the central case; and consult basic textbooks on the field of law in order to gain an insight into it. Counsel must remember that he will not have time to read all the texts and should make decisions as to which sources are important enough to research in depth.

During research, counsel should take notes on authorities that are relevant to the case. Scots law is based on principles of law. Relevant principles must be identified and noted during research as these provide an argument with weight. Always remember that the right answer is not in a book. Counsel must make the argument based on research, analysis of that research and application of the principles to the moot problem. The following texts will provide a general feel for the area of law and often reveal further reading:

Criminal Law Moot

Gordon, *The Criminal Law of Scotland* (3rd edn, 2005)
Hume, *Commentaries on the Law of Scotland Respecting Crimes*

---

[5] See Chapter 5 below.
[6] It is important to take notes for making rebuttals as discussed in para 4.8 below.

Contractual Law Moot

McBryde, *The Law of Contract in Scotland* (3rd edn, 2007)

Delict Law Moot

Thomson, *Delictual Liability* (4th edn, 2009)

Family Law Moot

Clive, *The Law of Husband and Wife in Scotland* (4th edn, 1997)

Company Law Moot

Davies, *Glower & Davies Principles of Modern Company Law* (8th edn, 2008)

All moots

Stair, *Institutions of the Law of Scotland*
Bell, *Commentaries on the Law of Scotland*
Stair Memorial Encyclopaedia

Identifying the Central Moot Points

Once basic research has been done the next tasks are to re-read the **3.4** problem and identify the central points to be argued. There will be several possible points to argue. However, there will only ever be one or two central issues that are at the heart of the moot. The central issues normally revolve around establishing the scope or nature of a particular law such that it can be applied to the facts.

The problem page may contain the points of law on which the parties are appealing. The points of law given for appeal may be side issues or may be poorly phrased such that they will have to be 'unpacked' and reworded to convey the centre of the legal issue.

The best counsel will cut to the heart of the issue and identify the central moot point. This may take several attempts. Often counsel will invest hours of research into one argument only to reach a dead end and change to another – do not be put off. It is sometimes possible to identify the central issue only by painstakingly eliminating all the side issues. In a real legal case all the side issues would be pleaded in order to try to win the case. In a moot, counsel have only minutes to make their client's case. Therefore, only the strongest arguments around the central issue should be brought to court.

In the majority of moots both parties will identify the same moot points and argue directly against each other. However, if a team has analysed the problem poorly and not found the issue of debate then they may end up arguing a side issue. In this event, the respondents should not argue against a point that has not been appealed by the appellants.[7] For this reason it is useful to be aware of arguments that could arise from side issues. Once the central points of law have been identified by counsel it is time for counsel to allocate tasks.

Allocation of Points of Law and Team Work

3.5   It is advisable for different points of law to be argued by each counsel. Senior counsel speaks for longer than junior counsel and should deal with the more complicated points of law. Utilising this technique allows each counsel to do in-depth research and specialise in a specific point of law that will be argued. However, this strategy requires counsel to trust each other's ability to research a point of law alone. Every year mooting teams drop out of competitions because one counsel has not done the work required for the moot. Remember to work as a team. Although researching different lines of argument each counsel should be kept abreast of what research is being done and how much progress has been made. Despite looking at different points of law it is still highly beneficial for counsel to discuss ideas and potential arguments together. Remember to support and encourage each other. It is important before the moot that counsel of the same team run through each other's arguments to ensure that there are no contradictions. Once the points of law have been allocated it is time for counsel to start substantive research into the law and start constructing a legal argument.

Summary

3.6   This chapter has:

1. established the method to be used for the first approach to a moot problem;
2. outlined what to identify when reading the moot problem;
3. provided guidance on researching the moot problem;
4. provided guidance on identifying the central moot points; and
5. identified the importance of team work and the need to allocate different points of law to different counsel.

---

[7] See para 11.3 below.

Chapter 4

STAGE 2: MAKING A LEGAL ARGUMENT

Introduction

There are many ways to make a successful legal argument. In court, an **4.1** argument must convey the point desired in a way simple enough for it to be understood. One of the key skills developed by taking part in a moot is how to make a good legal argument.

This chapter addresses stage 2: Making a Legal Argument. Stage 2 teaches competitors how to make a structured argument that the judge can follow. This chapter builds on the outline of the roles of counsel in Chapter 2. As such it will be useful to read this chapter in conjunction with para 2.3 above.

This chapter deals with: counsel's introduction; outlining the facts; putting a question to the court; making a submission; structuring a submission and an argument; and forming a good conclusion. This chapter also deals with rebuttals and hypothetical situations. Figure 3 below outlines the structure of stage 2 and provides references to the relevant sections of Chapter 4 that deal with each part of making the argument.

Figure 3   Stage 2: Making a Legal Argument

Stage 2: Making a Legal Argument	Reference
Introduction	para 4.2
Outlining the facts	para 4.3
Putting a question to the court	para 4.4
Submissions	para 4.5
Stating the structure of the argument/addressing the submission	para 4.6
Forming a concrete conclusion	para 4.7

A Good Introduction

4.2   Counsel should first introduce himself and state who counsel is representing. Counsel should then proceed to address the facts of the case.

> ### Example 1: Counsel's introduction
>
> *'Good evening My Lord. If it pleases Your Lordship my name is John Smith and I am junior counsel for the appellant Mr Calderwood.'*

Outlining the Facts

4.3   Junior counsel for the appellant must offer the judge a brief synopsis of the facts of the case at first instance in case the judge has not had time to read the moot problem.[8] It is not mandatory for any other counsel to offer the facts of the case at first instance. However, after counsel's introduction it may be useful for counsel to highlight relevant or important facts to the argument he is making.

> ### Example 2: Use of important facts
>
> *'John maliciously … HIT STEVEN OVER THE HEAD with a toothbrush.'*

Emphasising the assault and playing down the fact that a toothbrush was used can point out to the judge facts that are relevant to the argument counsel is making while playing down facts which may weaken counsel's argument.

Putting a Question to the Court

4.4   After counsel has outlined any relevant facts, counsel should tell the judge what is being argued before the court and what decision counsel wants the judge to hold in his judgment. Counsel will state what is being argued by putting a question to the court. Counsel will then proceed to state what counsel wants the judge to hold by stating his submissions. Essentially counsel puts a question to the court and then models his submissions and argument on how he thinks the question should be answered. This allows counsel to effectively set out the steps of his argument. Outlining the structure of the argument in this manner will show the judge how to proceed from the question asked of him to counsel's desired answer.

---

[8] See para 7.7 below.

Example 3: Putting the question to the court

After counsel introduces himself (and junior counsel gives the facts) he then puts the question to the court:

'My Lord the question before the court this evening is: Did the Grinch commit the act of theft in the early hours of the 25th of December?'

Having stated the question, counsel then models his submissions on how he thinks the question should be answered.

Submissions

A submission is a claim that counsel puts forward for consideration by the judge. Counsel will craft his central submissions with a view to answering the question that counsel has put to the court. Counsel's whole argument will be based on one or two central submissions. An expert counsel will take time to carefully craft clearly worded submissions. In doing so he will never lose sight of what he is arguing. **4.5**

Example 4: A basic submission

'I submit to Your Lordship that the Grinch did not commit theft as the required actus reus of appropriation was not committed, and as such my client is innocent.'

Having made this submission, counsel would then craft the rest of his argument with a view to establishing that his submission should be accepted as correct by the judge. The judge will either agree or disagree with counsel's submission at the end of the moot. The skilled counsel will craft a submission in such a way that the judge can lift the exact wording of the submission into his judgment.

When presenting submissions it is important to speak very slowly and clearly as the judge will be writing down what is being said verbatim. Watch the judge's pen carefully to make sure he writes down each submission. It may be beneficial to repeat the submission two or three times to ensure that the judge has heard it. If the judge has not written down counsel's submission then he may struggle to remember it after hearing complex arguments over the period of the moot. If the judge has forgotten counsel's submission then he has forgotten the point of counsel's argument.

It is hard enough for the judge to unpack a complicated but well presented argument. It is substantially harder for the judge to unpack a poorly presented submission in order to work out what counsel is arguing for in the first place.

> **Remember:** craft submissions clearly and carefully.

Having introduced himself, addressed the facts of the case, put the question to the court and stated his submission, counsel would then outline the structure of his argument.

Structuring an Argument

4.6 After the submission is made it is time to outline the structure of the argument showing how counsel intends to support the submission. Presenting the structure of the argument to the judge achieves two things. First, from the beginning the judge will be fully aware of the structure of counsel's argument and the judge will bear this in mind all the way through counsel's submission. This will ensure both counsel and the judge will not lose sight of what is being argued and why. Second, the outline used at the beginning of counsel's argument can be re-established in the conclusion or at any point during the argument thus reminding the judge of counsel's whole argument in a few lines.[9]

In the example below the moot point is whether the definition of 'appropriation' in the crime of theft covers the actions taken by the accused. The submission is the same submission used in example 4. It is restated below.

Example 5: Structuring an argument

'I submit to your lordship that the Grinch did not commit theft as the required actus reus of appropriation was not committed, and as such my client is innocent.'

After the submission is made the structure of the argument is given demonstrating how counsel will support the submission:

'In order to support this submission I intend to establish the test for theft. Once I have established the test, I will cite weighty authority to establish the scope of the actus reus. I will then apply the test to the facts of the case before us. An application of the test to the facts of the case will reveal that

---

[9] See para 4.7 below.

the actus reus of appropriation cannot be established, thus showing that the respondent is innocent.'

> **Remember:** structure is a consideration the judge takes into account when marking the performance of counsel.

Once the structure of the argument has been given counsel simply follows his own structure when making the argument. In this case counsel would proceed to establish a test for theft, cite authority and apply the test to the case before him. He would then conclude his submission. If he has another submission to make he will turn to his next submission. Once counsel has addressed all his submissions then counsel will conclude his argument.

Forming a Concrete Conclusion

When concluding it is appropriate to reiterate the structure of the argument given. Counsel should use the conclusion to make sure that the judge has fully understood all the points that have been argued and how they link together to support counsel's case. Counsel should not tell the judge that a principle has been established in his argument if counsel has tried to establish the principle but failed to do so during the moot. It may be useful to put a memorable phrase into the conclusion. An ideally drafted conclusion will be so well constructed that the judge will be able to lift an extract from the conclusion into his judgment. The judge will use the conclusion as an opportunity to reflect on the points that have been made and how the argument has been presented and structured. As such, counsel should put considerable thought into the conclusion and make sure the last thing that is said to the judge leaves him thinking kindly of counsel's case.

4.7

Example 6: A structured conclusion

'In conclusion My Lord, I have presented an authoritative definition for the crime of theft. I have analysed its application to the facts and have established that the actus reus of appropriation cannot be applied to a calendar event which cannot be physically taken. As such I submit to your lordship that my client, the Grinch, did not commit the act of theft and is as such innocent.'

In this example the judge will easily be able to lift the words, '*a calendar event cannot be physically taken*', into his judgment. He may state, '*In my opinion the law of Scotland is settled on the issue. It is clear that a calendar event cannot physically be taken.'*

Making a Rebuttal

4.8   Making a rebuttal can be done at any point during counsel's address to the court. Rebutting an opponent's submission means attempting to counteract it by providing reasoning. In short, counsel is stating that his version of the law is right and his opponent's version is wrong. It is up to counsel at what point rebuttals are made. Some counsel find that expressly starting with rebuttals can provide a bold impact in their argument. Other counsel prefer to point them out as they work through their argument. The best counsel will use a rebuttal as an opportunity to strengthen his argument by making the alternative look unattractive to the judge.

Counsel will not know what the opposition will be arguing until the moot takes place. This means that to make a rebuttal counsel must think on the spot and be confident to offer a rebuttal. Many competitors find this very hard. For this reason a judge will be very impressed by a good rebuttal. It is important during research to prepare rebuttals to arguments that are likely to be made by the opposition.

Rebutting a case or statute

In order to rebut a case that the opponents have cited counsel must distinguish it on one of many grounds. Distinguishing a case means separating it from the current case before the judge. To do this a competitor must give a reason why the case should not apply or why it is irrelevant.

A case can be irrelevant or should not apply if:

1. It is factually different from the case before the judge.
2. Counsel has cited another case that overrules that case.
3. It raises a different point of law from the case currently before the judge.
4. It is at odds with settled Scots law.
5. A dissenting judgment has been cited as authoritative.
6. The judge has stated the reasoning given is unique to the facts of that case.

A statute can be irrelevant if:

1. The statute has been amended or repealed by another statute.

2. The statute deals with a different point or field of law from the current case.

3. The statute does not apply in Scotland.

Even if a case does not set down a binding precedent it may still be persuasive. Equally an English statute that does not apply in Scotland can have persuasive authority if the field of Scots law being debated is based on English law.[10]

Example 7: A basic rebuttal

If the opponent outlines an out of date definition, counsel could rebut by stating:

*'My Lord I would like to make a short rebuttal. The learned junior counsel for the appellant has accurately and correctly outlined **a** definition for the crime of theft. However the case in which the definition was outlined has been overruled by the case of Black against Carmichael. As such I will now cite the most up to date and **valid** definition of theft from Black against Carmichael.'*

Hypothetical Situations

Hypothetical situations can be presented at any point during counsel's address to the court. They are useful for highlighting a factual point or for evaluating how a legal principle could be applied to a factual situation. Counsel must make the judge aware that a hypothetical situation is being presented.   **4.9**

Example 8: Introducing a hypothetical situation

'With your lordship's permission I now wish to demonstrate the principle 'a calendar event cannot be stolen' by application of the principle to a hypothetical scenario' (Judge nods), 'Supposing, hypothetically, the Grinch had attempted to steal Tuesday on the 24th of December and not the well known event, Christmas.'

Summary

This chapter has: **4.10**

1. built on the outline of the roles of counsel in Chapter 2;

---

[10] See para 5.6 below.

2. demonstrated how to make a structured legal argument that the judge will be able to follow;
3. addressed how to make a good introduction;
4. dealt with how to outline the facts of the case and put a question to the court;
5. addressed how to make a submission and how to structure an argument;
6. demonstrated how to make a good conclusion; and
7. explored the use of hypothetical situations and rebuttals.

Chapter 5

USE OF AUTHORITY

Introduction

Authority is vital when making a legal argument. Judges and counsel use authoritative sources to ensure that a statement made about the law is accurate and correct. The correct use of authority in a moot is of fundamental importance. This chapter addresses definition of authority; the reason for citing authority; court etiquette and speaking skills required when citing authority; the relevance or weight that authority has; and different types of authority. It also provides guidance on the importance of providing a list of authority the day before a moot, how to put authority in a folder for the clerk; and giving correct citations of authority for the clerk. **5.1**

Definition of Authority

Authority is a reliable source of information that provides counsel's argument with weight. No claim can be made about the law without support from *legal authority*. The more reliable the source the more authority it carries. Providing authority in a moot is the equivalent of saying: 'Do not listen to my version of the law for I am an unreliable law student. Listen to Lord Hope's reliable version of the law in his judgment in the case of McDonald against Her Majesty's Advocate.[11] It is likely he will know what he is talking about.' **5.2**

Citing Authority

Citing authority in a moot involves showing the judge exactly where the law can be found. A judge has to physically see the words on the page to know that counsel is not making up the law. For that reason, to cite authority counsel *must* bring the judge's attention directly to the **5.3**

---

[11] 2008 SLT 993.

exact words that provide weight for counsel's argument. Many students attempt to circumvent poor understanding of a case by citing the whole case as authority for a proposition. Stating a whole case report or textbook as authority for a proposition is incorrect. Part of being a good advocate is being able to find the exact sentence, section and ratio that is authority for your proposition. Although counsel will need to understand the law in great depth, counsel will only ever need to cite a few paragraphs of authority to the judge.

> **Remember:** only words used by the judge can be cited in authority.

Etiquette when Citing Authority to a Judge

5.4   Counsel must follow an established method of citing authority to a judge or risk being penalised by the judge. There are five points that counsel must remember in order to correctly cite authority.

1. Counsel must tell the judge why the authority is being cited

The judge will want to know what makes this authority relevant to the argument counsel is making.

Example 9: Explanation for citation

'My Lord, this case establishes a persuasive legal test for the common law crime of plegium.'

2. If the authority is a case then counsel must offer the judge the facts of the case and any other relevant information

The judge will always expect counsel to offer him the facts of a case as a matter of courtesy. If counsel states that the case is being cited primarily for the point of law and not the facts then the judge may choose not to hear them.

Example 10: Offering the facts

'Does Your Lordship require a brief synopsis of the facts of this case?' or

'It is worth noting that the facts of the case are not materially tied to the point of law decided. However I am prepared to provide Your Lordship with a brief synopsis of the case if necessary.'

3. Counsel must bring the judge to the exact sentence and word being cited

When counsel cites authority he must bring the judge to the exact word being cited. If citing to a judge from a case report then counsel must state the name of the judge counsel is citing from and whether the judgment being quoted is assenting or dissenting. As a fundamental issue counsel should not abbreviate parties' names or use letters instead of words when giving a citation. Counsel should give a full citation and be aware if a case cited is being argued by His or Her Majesty's Advocate. Failure to give a full citation will be heavily criticised.

> **Example 11: Full citation**
>
> *'If Your Lordship would turn his attention to the case of Her Majesty's Advocate against Millar or Oates, reported in the eighteen-sixty-two volume four of Irvine's Justiciary Reports, at page seventy-nine. I am reading from Lord Ardmillan's assenting opinion, the fourth paragraph down, eight lines down from the top of the paragraph, beginning 'He concurred with Lord Cowan.' Does your lordship have the relevant passage?'*
>
> Counsel should not state:
>
> *'HMA vee Millar in the 1862 Iee 4 at 79.'*

4. Counsel must give the judge plenty of time

When quoting, counsel must make sure the judge has time to listen, read, understand and write. This means pausing, repeating and speaking abnormally slowly. Counsel must watch the judge closely when quoting to ensure that his needs are being catered for. Many competitors lose points when quoting to the judge by not taking their time and not making sure the judge is following them. It cannot be stressed enough that the skill of catering for the judge is what separates the winners from the losers. Counsel must hold the judge's attention and guide him through counsel's citation and argument. It may be beneficial for counsel to deliberately pause during or after a quote to let the judge think. Most judges want to question a counsel's understanding of the quote. This is an ideal place for counsel to make a good impression by showing familiarity and confidence with the material cited.

5. Counsel must give a translation if quoting a language other than English

If quoting in a foreign language, for example Latin, counsel is required to give a translation into English.

Example 12: Quoting Latin

'My Lord the legal maxim 'Volenti non fit injuria', 'No wrong is done to one who consents', applies in this case.'

Relevance of Authority

5.5   Counsel should try to get the most relevant and authoritative source of the principle he is citing. There are two factors that will affect the relevance of authority.

1. The source of the authority.
2. The application of the authority to the current case.

The two factors must be balanced. A case may be very authoritative but may not be relevant. A House of Lords case will be of little authority if it is not in point with the current case. Equally if a Sheriff Court case is factually similar to the case before the judge then it will be highly relevant and thus worth citing although not binding.

Different Types of Authority

5.6   New competitors often ask the question, 'What can be used as authority?' Authority can come in a variety of forms.

Scottish Authority

Judges look to the law of Scotland before considering authority from a foreign legal system. There will often be a large volume of Scottish authority on the problem. The most reliable sources are statutes, case law, institutional works and possibly leading textbooks. When citing a case, use the most highly regarded case reports. For example, reports in the Session Cases, ahead of those in the *Scots Law Times*, ahead of those in Scottish Criminal Case Reports. All recent judgments are now published on the official webpages of the Scottish Courts (www.scotcourts.gov.uk) but should be cited by the case reference given there rather than the URL.

If the account of a case is considered to be unofficial then a judge may not give much weight to it. Do not cite a student textbook, newspaper, dictionary or a web page. The judge will not consider the source to be a reliable depiction of Scots law.

> **Remember:** judges will consider use of authority carefully when assessing the mooting performance so counsel should use the most reliable authority available.

Foreign Authority

It is useful to look to a foreign legal system if there is no Scottish authority for the point of law being debated. It is important to remember that foreign law is never binding in Scotland and has only a persuasive value. The level of its value will depend upon how in point it is with the current case.

English law may be uniquely useful. An English case will be in point if it is on the interpretation of a statute that applies in both England and Scotland. As such it may carry some authority where Scots law is silent on the issue. Counsel should preface citation of foreign law with an acknowledgement that it is only persuasive.

> **Remember:** foreign law is not binding in Scotland.

Aged Authority

Cases can be overruled. Statutes can be amended. Textbooks can be out-of-date. Counsel should check that the law being cited is still reliable and authoritative. For example, an extract from an institutional writing which condemned homosexual relations would be considered to be an out-of-date source today. Out-of-date authority may still be useful if counsel is trying to argue that the law should revert to an earlier state, or where it is relevant to the argument to trace the development of the law.

Providing a List of Authorities to the Judge, Clerk and Opposing Team

Counsel are required to produce a list of authorities they wish to cite at a specified time (usually one day) before the moot takes place. A copy must

5.7

be given to the judge, the clerk and the opposing team.[12] This means that limited time is available to read the authorities given by the opponents and to prepare rebuttals.

Many counsel leave the exact page from which they will draw out of their citations to make it harder for the opposition to predict their argument. The opponent may be put off trying to find the ratio in a lengthy case report. However, counsel should remember that the judge and clerk will need extra time to find the correct page during the moot.

Although counsel will only have time to cite a handful of authorities to the judge many counsel consider it an advantage to have a large variety of authorities cited and brought to the moot. Counsel may be able to make use of extra authority in a spontaneous rebuttal if counsel knows the authorities well.

When counsel gives a citation in his list of authorities the clerk will get the exact text cited for the moot. For example, if counsel cited the Sale of Goods Act 1979, c 54 then the clerk would get a copy of the public general statutes for 1979 and hand it opened at chapter 54 to the judge. If counsel wanted to cite the Sale of Goods Act 1979, c 54 as amended by the Sale of Goods (Amendment) Act 1994 c 32 then counsel must cite that in his list of authorities, so that an amended version is produced from current law statutes or official publications. Counsel should ensure that the citation for a case used in the list of authorities is the same report version as that from which counsel will be working in the moot, eg that both are the Session Cases report.

Remember: what counsel cites is what counsel gets.

Putting Authority in a Folder for the Clerk

5.8   It is becoming more common for counsel to photocopy relevant authority and place it in a folder for the clerk. This is advantageous as it allows counsel to highlight or underline relevant sections of text. Counsel must inform the clerk before the moot that counsel will be citing from a folder in order to prevent the clerk reaching for books during the moot. When directing the judge to authority in a folder counsel should remember to give the full citation first and then state where in the folder it can be found.[13] It is useful to put a table of contents in the front of the folder.

---

[12] The Aberdeen University Law Mooting Society will organise this for competitors of its competitions.

[13] See para 13.4 below.

Example 13: Citing from a folder

'If Your Lordship would turn his attention to the case of Her Majesty's Advocate against Millar or Oates, reported in the 1862 volume 4 of Irvine's Justiciary Reports, at page 79. I am reading from Lord Ardmillan's assenting opinion, the 4th paragraph down, 8 lines down from the top beginning, 'He concurred with Lord Cowan', which can be found at tab 4 of the red folder'.

Citation Guide

A guide on the correct format of citations for the list of authorities is provided below.[14]   **5.9**

Books:	Author's name, title of book, date of publication, edition number.
Cases:	Pursuer v Defender, year, reports, page.
Statutes:	Short title
Institutional Works:	Book number, title, section

Example 14: Different citations

Gordon, *The Criminal Law of Scotland* (3rd edn, 2005)

Black v Carmichael 1992 SLT 897

Sale of Goods Act 1979

Stair, 1, 7, 4

Summary

This chapter has: **5.10**

1. provided a definition of authority;
2. given reasons why authority is cited at a moot;
3. addressed the required court etiquette and speaking skills for citing authority;
4. discussed the relevance of authority;
5. examined different types of authority;
6. addressed providing a list of authority to the judge, clerk and opposing team;

---

[14] See the Oxford Standard for Citation of Legal Authorities available online at < http://denning.law.ox.ac.uk/published/oscola_2006.pdf>.

7. analysed how to put authority in a folder for the clerk; and

8. provided a guide to giving correct citations of authority to the clerk.

Chapter 6

USE OF TIME

Introduction

Alongside the use of authority in mooting competitions another common **6.1** area of difficulty for mooting competitors is time management. It is difficult to get a flowing and dynamic argument to finish at exactly the right time, leaving no time wasted, while not incurring the penalty for running over the time limit. This chapter aims to help competitors to correctly manage the time available. This chapter deals with: time management; factors that counsel needs to be aware will affect the time available; and good methods for improving time management.

Time Management

Counsel must attempt to craft his submissions such that counsel's argument **6.2** finishes within the time allowed. The clerk will keep time and will notify counsel by holding up a notice or ringing a bell when counsel has two minutes left, one minute left and when time has run out. If counsel runs over time then counsel must state to the judge that time has run out and request a minute to conclude.

Example 15: Apologising for running over the time limit

'My Lord, it appears I have run out of time. With Your Lordship's permission may I have a moment to conclude my argument?'

Counsel should not continue talking after time is up without asking the judge's permission. The purpose of limiting time in a moot is to teach counsel to make a concise argument. Running over the time limit demonstrates to the judge that counsel lacks this vital skill.

> **Remember:** the judge will consider time management in his marking.

Factors Affecting Time

6.3 When judging how much time is available to make submissions counsel should take account of the following:

1. If citing authority counsel must allow time for the clerk and judge to find the page.
2. If the judge is taking extensive notes counsel must speak more slowly to cater for this.
3. If the judge questions counsel then counsel must stop and give an answer. For this counsel may need to consult with counsel's partner.[15]
4. If one of counsel's arguments falls through counsel may need time to reorganise on the spot.
5. If the judge requests the facts of all cases cited to him this may take more time.

It is very difficult to work out exactly how long counsel's argument has to be. Thus, it is vitally important that counsel practises the timing of delivering the argument. Counsel must limit the length of submissions so that he can allow enough time for unforeseen circumstances.

Good Methods of Time Management

6.4

1. It is most useful to isolate a section of argument such that it can be added on to an existing argument if there is extra time, or it can be extracted from the argument if there is insufficient time available.
2. It is advisable that counsel prepares and rehearses a strong conclusion to the argument that can be deployed at any point after two thirds of the argument has been delivered. This allows counsel to produce a structured conclusion even if time has run out.
3. Counsel should rehearse and time his argument beforehand, being prepared to modify it if necessary. Counsel should practice changing the argument on the spot to account for time problems. Doing this will give counsel a feel for which parts of the argument can be dropped if necessary. Counsel should practise speaking slowly when making a submission or directing the judge to a citation and a quotation.

---

[15] Some competitions allow extra time for dealing with questions.

Remember: rehearsing the speech out loud is the most important part of preparation for a moot. It will increase self-confidence and the fluency of the argument.

Summary

This chapter has: **6.5**

1. provided guidance on how to correctly manage the time available to competitors;
2. addressed factors that counsel should be aware will affect the time available to make counsel's argument; and
3. provided guidance on good methods for improving counsel's time-management skills.

Chapter 7

COURT ETIQUETTE

Introduction

The court etiquette in a moot is similar to the style of etiquette used in **7.1**
a real court. Counsel must address the court correctly and good counsel
will develop this skill naturally. The judge will expect correct court
etiquette and will penalise incorrect etiquette. This chapter aims to teach
counsel the correct court address for a moot court. This chapter deals
with: addressing the judge; referring to counsel including the opponents
and partners; general court address; and the required etiquette for taking
and leaving the lectern. This chapter also addresses the requirement for
senior counsel for the appellant to introduce all counsel at the beginning
of the moot and the requirement for junior counsel for the appellant to
offer the judge the facts of the case at first instance.

Addressing the Judge

The judge is addressed in the third person. Counsel must stand when **7.2**
addressing the judge.

A male judge is referred to as 'My Lord', 'Your Lordship' (in the place of
you), and 'Your Lordship's' (in the place of you're).

Example 16: Referring to a male judge

*'My Lord, it is clear to me that on Your Lordship's right, Your Lordship will
find the relevant book.'*

A female judge is referred to as 'My Lady' or 'Your Ladyship' (in the place
of you), and 'Your Ladyship's' (in the place of you're).

Example 17: Referring to a female judge

*'My Lady, it is clear to me that on Your Ladyship's right, Your Ladyship
will find the relevant book.'*

A male panel of judges or a mixed sex panel of judges is referred to as 'My Lords', 'Your Lordships' (in the place of you and you're).

Example 18: Referring to a male or mixed panel of judges

'My Lords, it is clear to me that on Your Lordships' right, Your Lordships will find the clerk of the court.'

A female panel of judges is referred to as 'My Ladys', 'Your Ladyships' (in the place of you and you're).

Example 19: Referring to a female panel of judges

'My Ladys, it is clear to me that on Your Ladyships' right, Your Ladyships will find the clerk of the court.'

When addressing the judge counsel should begin by stating 'If it pleases Your Lordship' or 'Thank you, My Lord'.

Example 20: Addressing the judge

'If it pleases Your Lordship I would like to move to my second submission' (judge nods), *'Thank you My Lord, I submit that …'*

Referring to Counsel

7.3　Counsel should refer to the opponents as 'My learned friend, junior/senior counsel for the appellant/respondent' or 'My learned friend opposite'.[16]

Example 21: Referring to the opponent

'With great respect to my learned friend senior counsel for the appellant, the field of law has been inaccurately depicted'

Counsel should refer to his partner as 'My learned senior/junior'.

Example 22: Referring to counsel's partner

'As my learned junior has already discussed the case of Black against Carmichael I shall now move to discuss the case of Her Majesty's Advocate against Millar or Oates.'

General Court Address

7.4　Counsel should not state 'I think that the law is' as this is only an opinion on the law. Counsel should make submissions to the court stating clearly what the law is.

---

[16] In practice, much of a case will be negotiated between counsel. It is preferable to remain on good terms with the opposing counsel.

Example 23: Making a submission

'I submit that the law should be reformed.'

At the end of counsel's argument it is correct to invite the judge to ask questions on the points argued.

Example 24: Inviting the judge to ask questions

'That, My Lord, concludes the arguments I wish to submit on behalf of the appellant. Perhaps there are some issues on which I may be of further assistance?'

To conclude counsel's argument counsel should thank the judge.

Example 25: Thanking the judge

'I am obliged, My lord' or 'Thank you, My lord.'

Taking and Leaving the Lectern

Senior counsel for the appellant will have already introduced all other counsel to the judge. However, out of etiquette when taking the lectern counsel should introduce himself again before addressing the judge. **7.5**

Example 26: Counsel introducing himself

'Good evening My Lord. If it pleases Your Lordship my name is John Smith and I am senior counsel for the respondent.'

Normally, the judge will thank counsel and nod when he is satisfied that counsel's argument is concluded. Counsel should not walk away from the judge without the judge acknowledging that counsel can leave. Counsel should give a small bow to the judge when stepping away from the lectern as a mark of respect to the court.

Senior Counsel's Introduction

At the beginning of the moot the judge will state: 'Who appears?' At this point senior counsel for the appellant will introduce the respondent's junior then senior counsel and the appellant's junior counsel then himself. **7.6**

Example 27: Senior counsel's introduction

'Appearing for the respondent My Lord is Mr Alistair Fisher as junior counsel, and Mr Fredric Brown as senior counsel. Appearing for the appellant My Lord is Mrs Nicola Bell as junior counsel, and I, Mr James Crawford as senior counsel.'

Senior counsel must speak very slowly and watch the judge's pen as the judge will be writing the names of the competitors down verbatim for use throughout the moot.

Junior Counsel's Offer of the Facts

7.7   The judge will request junior counsel for the appellant to speak first. After introducing himself he must offer a brief description of the facts of the case before the judge at first instance. Essentially, this is a brief synopsis of the problem. It is unusual for the judge to accept junior counsel's offer. However, if he does, junior counsel must be prepared to provide a consolidated version of the case being discussed.

Example 28: Junior counsel's offer of the facts

'Before I begin, does your lordship require a brief synopsis of the case at first instance?'

Summary

7.8   This chapter has:

1. addressed the court etiquette used in mooting competitions;
2. provided guidance on how to address the judge;
3. set out how to refer to counsel;
4. addressed the required etiquette for taking and leaving the lectern;
5. addressed the requirement for senior counsel for the appellant to introduce all other counsel; and
6. addressed the requirement for junior counsel for the appellant to offer the judge the facts of the case at first instance.

Chapter 8

TEAM TACTICS AND STRATEGIES

Introduction

This chapter analyses strategies that are commonly deployed by competitors in the moot court. Some of these examples may seem complicated to the first time competitor. It is advisable that this chapter be read when counsel is familiar with the structure of legal tests and how they are established and applied. This chapter deals with: choosing which submissions should be made by which counsel; using red herrings on authority lists; the act of conceding submissions; and the reverse ordering of submissions. Each of these strategies requires good team work.

8.1

Choosing which Counsel Makes which Submissions

Junior counsel for the appellant has the advantage of talking first. This means that he can establish any ground he likes for appeal. Normally, because of the nature of the problem, there will be only a few possible submissions to make. However, the more creative junior counsel's submissions are, the more surprised the respondents will be.

8.2

Junior counsel for the respondent is first in line to respond to the appellant's arguments. This means junior counsel for the respondent will have only minutes to adjust his argument to counter any unexpected submissions. A properly prepared responding team will know the area of law well enough to predict what grounds the appellant will be appealing on and consequently the submissions of the appellant.

Senior counsel for the appellant has the difficult job of trying to complete the arguments for the appellant while anticipating all possible counter-arguments that the senior counsel for the respondent (who will speak last) could make. As senior counsel has the last word for the appellant he must make an effort to defend against all possible rebuttals in his own submissions.

Senior counsel for the respondent has the advantage that the appellants will have already developed their case and as such will be unable to rebut his arguments. The disadvantage is that the points of law being discussed may have moved away from what senior counsel for the respondent will have researched and prepared. In this case, counsel must adapt his argument and potentially speak off the cuff. This is where the real talent in mooting lies and the judge will appreciate a good performance in this regard.

The Red Herring

8.3 Both teams are required to submit authorities before the moot. The 'red herring' is simply where counsel put cases into their list of authorities which they do not intend to use. This means the opponents will spend time looking up the cases and reading them while trying to anticipate why counsel intend to cite them. This wastes the opponents' time and can confuse them. Putting red herrings into the list of authorities is considered bad etiquette and is frowned upon. The judge will also have to read the authorities and he will not be impressed if counsel wastes his time with a red herring.

Conceding Submissions

8.4 Conceding a submission means accepting that a submission already made is incorrect and thus that the opposing team's counter-submission is correct. It is a good strategy for the appellants to invent an irrelevant submission just to concede it later on thus confusing the respondents. It is difficult for counsel for the respondent to concede a submission as doing so is a poor way of responding to a case against his client. However, it may be a good tactical decision to abandon a submission against one point to focus on another point.

Thus, for example: if in order for there to be a breach of contract there first has to be a contract to breach then it may be a good idea to argue only that the breach of contract did not happen and concede that a contract was created. This avoids arguing the more difficult argument that the contract was not created. Conceding a submission in this manner provides more time for counsel to argue that the contract was not breached. However, this involves counsel's entire case hanging on one point and is a risky strategy.

Example 29: Conceding a submission

'My Lord it is conceded by the appellant that a contract was formed by the signing of the document. However I submit to Your Lordship that the appellant's actions did not amount to a breach of contract.'

Reversing the Order of Submissions

This section deals with a specific question raised by competitors acting as **8.5** counsel for the respondent. What happens when counsel has prepared to respond to a point that has not yet been appealed?

A moot may hang on two moot points. If point two depends upon point one being established then the logical order of argument would be to establish point one and then move on to point two. For example: in order for there to be a breach of a contract, there must first be a contract to breach.

In this case it is logical that junior counsel for the appellant will try to establish that there is a contract and then senior counsel for the appellant will try to establish that there has been a breach of that contract. The respondents probably will have prepared junior counsel to counter-argue that there is no contract and senior counsel to counter-argue that there was no breach of the contract.

However, if junior counsel for the appellant attempts to establish that there was a breach of contract and states that his senior will try to establish that there was a contract then when junior counsel for the respondent makes his argument he may feel unable to respond to the argument that there is a contract as the appellants have not attempted to establish there is a contract yet.

If the appellants reverse their submissions it confuses the respondents and has been known to cause havoc with past counsel.

To respond to this, junior counsel for the respondent should simply make his submissions and then state that his senior counsel will deal with responding to the issue of whether there is a breach of contract which has just been made by junior counsel for the appellant. Then junior counsel should state that he will argue the issue of whether or not there was a contact. Counsel must remember to tell the judge he is arguing in this order because there cannot be a breach of contract unless there was first a contract, and thus if it cannot be established that there was a contract then a breach of it is entirely irrelevant. This should restructure the moot and give the respondents the upper hand again.

Top competitors will have prepared their submissions so well that they will have established that point one depends upon point two and thus will counter the reversing of the appellant's submissions by presenting a more structured and logical argument.

Summary

8.6 This chapter has:

1. addressed strategies that competitors use in the moot court;
2. addressed how to choose which submissions should be made by which counsel;
3. dealt with red herrings;
4. analysed the act of conceding submissions; and
5. analysed the reverse ordering of submissions.

Chapter 9

BODY LANGUAGE AND PRESENTATION SKILLS

Introduction

Possessing excellent presentation and body language skills makes listening to counsel's argument easy. In reality, counsel will have to practice hard to learn how to deploy good body language and presentation skills. This chapter provides advice on presentation and body language that will help develop these skills. This chapter addresses public speaking skills and body language including use of eye contact, physical movement and the use of the voice.

9.1

Public Speaking

Public speaking is a skill which is vital in mooting. One of the biggest advantages to mooting is the opportunity to develop public speaking skills in a mock court room setting. Counsel should speak loudly and clearly so the judge can hear. Counsel should speak slowly enough for the judge to understand. It may take a judge longer to understand because he has to listen and write at the same time. Counsel will need to compensate for being nervous by focusing on how he is speaking. At all times counsel should remember to speak to the judge and not to his notes. It is common for counsel to forget good presentation skills when put on the spot in a moot court. Counsel should remember to practice them and be aware of good public speaking skills during the moot.

9.2

Body Language

Eye Contact

9.3

In terms of body language it is important for counsel to make as much eye contact with the judge as is possible. The judge wants to see that counsel is paying attention to him. Counsel should not be afraid to make eye contact with the judge. In equal regard, counsel should not make the judge uncomfortable by staring into the judge's eyes for the whole presentation.

A judge will naturally award a counsel who makes good use of eye contact higher marks than an equal counsel who does not.

Physical Movement

Counsel should use hand movements and signals to emphasise his point. However, counsel should avoid fidgeting in front of the judge as this is very off-putting.

1. When pointing out the differences between two cases counsel may move his right hand while making a point about one case and then switch to moving his left hand to discuss the other.
2. When counsel wishes to place particular emphasis on a quote then he should raise both hands in the air.
3. By nodding and shaking his head counsel can provide a clear signal to the judge of his approval or disapproval on the point being discussed.
4. Counsel could lean in towards the lectern when dealing with a more important point and lean out from the lectern when dealing with side issues.
5. Counsel should not walk around the room or stray away from the lectern. This will attract a negative reaction from the judge who will not be able to focus on what is being said by counsel.

Use of the voice

Counsel may wish to vary the volume and tone of his voice. If something is important counsel should speak slowly, loudly and with emphasis on the words of importance.

These are just some of the tools that the excellent counsel will utilise successfully when making a presentation. However, counsel should use each of these tools in moderation. A judge may find excessive body language and use of speaking skills off-putting and may even struggle to follow counsel's argument.

> **Remember:** a moot is not a stage production; counsel should not be over-dramatic.

Summary

9.4   This chapter has:

1. addressed the need for excellent presentation and body language skills;
2. provided guidance on public speaking skills; and
3. provided guidance on the use of body language including the use of physical movement and use of the voice.

Chapter 10

THE JUDGE

Introduction

The judge is a phantom of fear for the first-time competitor. Although **10.1** a new competitor may have a good grasp of structuring an argument or may have good public speaking skills or extensive experience of public speaking, it is unlikely that new counsel will know what to expect from the judge. For this reason, this chapter examines what to expect when dealing with the judge and provides six points to remember when approaching the judge. This chapter addresses: the correct etiquette for addressing the judge to gain his respect; how to deal with the judge's questions; what to expect in the judge's judgment on the law and on the performance of the mooters. This chapter also provides a sample score sheet to show what the judge is looking for from counsel.

What to Expect from the Judge

The judge is a human volunteer. He may have not judged a moot before **10.2** and he may be as nervous as counsel. He may be a lecturer or he may be a judge from the Court of Session. In all cases the judge wants to hear counsel present counsel's argument in an understandable way. He will be aware that counsel is nervous and he may even make a joke to try to calm counsel down. Counsel should try to be at ease with him.

From the judge's perspective he will have to listen to over an hour of argument on a complex area of law without any breaks. The arguments made by the appellants and the respondents will not align perfectly as neither side knows in advance exactly what the other will argue. Counsel may have poor speaking skills and their arguments may be poorly structured. For these reasons, the judge may struggle to concentrate for the full time-period and judges may let their minds wander if counsel does not help them to focus.

Counsel should remember these points when approaching the judge:

1. He will lose interest in what is being said if it becomes too complicated to follow or is poorly delivered.
2. He wants the law explained as clearly as possible while giving him time to write things down.
3. He wants counsel to speak slowly enough and leave pauses such that he can think about what is being said.
4. He wants counsel to know the law clearly enough that when he asks a question about something counsel can give him an answer that makes sense and reassures him that he is in good hands with counsel explaining the law to him.
5. He does not want counsel to shout at him, patronise him or embarrass him in front of the audience.
6. Above all else, counsel should remember that the judge does not have the right answer hidden away under the table. He will have to decide the law based on what counsel argues.

As such it is counsel who has the right answer. That should fill counsel with confidence when talking to the judge.

Etiquette for Addressing the Judge

10.3   In court, a judge commands the respect of others. When he speaks others must stop and listen. He will listen to what counsel has to say if counsel commands his respect. To achieve this, counsel will need to prove to him that counsel is worth respecting. This is where etiquette comes into court work. Counsel should be confident, firm and address the judge with a professional air. Counsel should never speak off the cuff, never use foul language, and use humour sparingly. Counsel may well be addressing a real judge or law lord when doing a moot, who will expect counsel to endeavour to match court etiquette. Counsel should show him *respect* and *courtesy*. Counsel should be considerate of his needs; ensure he can hear what is being said and that he has time to write if he wishes to do so. Counsel should not apologise unless counsel has done something wrong; apologies make counsel appear in the wrong and, consequently, in a weak position. Finally, counsel should never talk over the top of a judge. If the judge is to be persuaded by counsel's argument he must first respect counsel.

Questions

10.4   The judge may at any time ask questions on the argument counsel is making. If counsel did not hear or understand the question it is appropriate to ask politely for it to be repeated. It is important that counsel thinks how to negotiate the answer before speaking. The judge will be looking for clarification on a point made that he has not understood or testing counsel's ability to respond to questions and think on the spot. This means the judge will be looking for counsel to adapt his legal argument to cater for the judge's perspective of the problem.

The best response is to address his question and tie the answer back to a piece of legal authority. This will allow you to use his question to build the strength of your argument. This may be the authority counsel is citing at the moment or counsel may inform the judge that he will deal with the point raised shortly when addressing another piece of authority. If the judge seems to be 'wrong' in his understanding of the law then counsel must be prepared to distinguish the issue that has arisen and inform the judge why his understanding is wrong.[17]

With questions, the more counsel prepares the better. If counsel has a sound understanding of the law and the facts of the case, counsel will normally be sufficiently prepared to answer any question. If counsel does not understand a case he is citing then he may have difficulty answering questions on it. When counsel is going over counsel's argument, counsel should try to spot the weak points of the argument or where things do not quite make sense. The judge will ask questions on the weak points of counsel's argument so counsel should be prepared to answer them in the moot.

The expert counsel will try to understand why the judge has asked the question in order to see how counsel's answer will affect the judge's understanding of the law being discussed. The judge may be asking a question in order to ascertain the reasoning behind the argument being made or in order to work out if he can extract a legal test from the answer.

A moot tests counsel's ability to make an argument. Counsel should *not* answer a question by telling the judge he 'does not know'. If counsel states that he does not know what he is arguing then counsel's argument will carry very little weight. This essentially forces the judge to accept the uncontested argument of the opposition. A good advocate, through reasoning, can make a respectable response to a question for which he has no answer.

Saying 'I think you mean' or 'I think it is' is the same as saying 'I don't really know, but it could be.' Counsel should not merely think he knows the answer, counsel should know the answer.

---

[17] See para 4.8 below.

If counsel genuinely cannot think of an answer to the question counsel may request permission to consult with counsel's junior or senior counsel. If junior counsel leaves a question to be addressed by his senior then senior counsel must ensure he deals with that question. If neither counsel knows the answer then counsel should simply inform the judge that counsel cannot take this point any further and request the judge's permission to move on with counsel's argument.

The Judge's Marking Criteria

10.5   The judge will take into account a number of factors when marking the performance of each counsel. The judge will consider counsel's analysis of the law and moot problem, use of court etiquette and speaking skills, response to the judge's questions, use of rebuttals, use of time, the structure of counsel's argument and the relevance of authority counsel has cited. However, it is at the complete discretion of the judge how he marks counsel and a judge may give more weight to a well-presented argument with poor knowledge of the law than a poorly-presented argument with a good knowledge of the law.

> **Remember:** the judge is looking for a good overall argument.

Figure 4   The Judge's Marking Criteria

	Junior Counsel for the Appellant	Senior Counsel for the Appellant	Junior Counsel for the Respondent	Senior Counsel for the Respondent
JUDGE'S SCORE SHEET				
NAMES				
Analysis of the Law and Moot Problem				
Structure of Argument and Team Work				
Relevance of Authority and Citation Skills				
Speaking Skills and use of Court Etiquette				
Response to Questions				
Effectiveness of Rebuttals				
Use of Time				
	Winners of the Law:	Appellant / Respondent		
	Winners of the Moot:	Appellant / Respondent		

The Judgment

Once senior counsel for the respondent has concluded his argument the judge will take a few minutes to collect his thoughts before delivering his judgment. His judgment will be bi-part in nature, first on the point of law, and second on the moot.

10.6

The law

The law will be awarded to one party. Judgment on the law will come in the form of an opinion similar to a case report but in a less developed form. Judgment on the law is an excellent opportunity for counsel who have performed thorough research to hear the honest opinion of a judge or legal practitioner on that field of law as it has been presented. The judge will often provide words of wisdom on the law of Scotland which can provide an insight into what is for many law students the hidden world of practising lawyers and judges.

The Moot

The moot will then be awarded to one party. The judge may comment on the performance of the counsel, of each individual counsel, and often summarise his thoughts on the whole moot before indicating which party has been successful. It is an invaluable opportunity for counsel to hear their successes and flaws in making and presenting legal argument. For counsel this is where the opportunity arises to make the whole process worthwhile by noting what has to be improved for the next moot, exam, public speaking event or indeed for arguing in later professional life.

Summary

This chapter has:

10.7

1. analysed six points that counsel should remember when dealing with the judge;
2. addressed the correct etiquette for gaining the judge's respect;
3. provided guidance on how to deal with the judge's questions;
4. addressed what to expect in the judge's judgment on the law and on the winners of the moot; and
5. provided a sample score sheet to show what the judge is marking counsel on.

Chapter 11

PROCEDURE ON THE DAY OF THE MOOT

Introduction

Each of the previous chapters has dealt with what to do in preparation for **11.1**
the moot. This chapter looks at the moot competition itself including: the
final preparations for the moot competition; the dress code required; and
the approach for when counsel arrives at the moot court. This chapter also
addresses the procedure of the moot, including what to do when the judge
enters the room, what to do before counsel makes his argument and what
to do thereafter.

Preparation

On the day of the moot, counsel should arrive at court early and dress in **11.2**
business-like clothing.[18] Counsel should take counsel's notes, a bottle of
water, two photocopies of each authority counsel is citing,[19] one copy of
his opponents authorities, paper to write on and utensils to write with.
Counsel will be given a court gown to wear at the moot. Counsel should
take counsel's respective seat and get acquainted with the surroundings.[20]
It is advisable for senior counsel for the appellant to write down the
names of all other counsel and their respective positions in preparation
for introducing them to the judge. The judge will often arrive last and only
a few minutes before the moot will start. The judge will arrange his papers
and then leave the room with the clerk.

The Moot

The organiser of the moot will then ensure that everyone is ready and **11.3**
introduce the moot competition. He will then let the clerk know that the

---

[18] Business dress is worn as a mark of respect for the judge and to create a professional
atmosphere. A suit is recommended or similar smart clothing.
[19] One copy is for the judge if for some reason the clerk does not have the authorities.
[20] See para 1.3 below.

moot can begin. The clerk will call the court to order by entering the room and shouting 'Court' at which point all must stand as a mark of respect as the judge re-enters the room.

The judge will sit down (at which point everyone else may sit) and state, 'Who appears?' Senior counsel for the appellants will stand and introduce himself and all other counsel. The judge will then invite junior counsel for the appellant to make his submissions, at which point junior counsel will proceed to the lectern and begin his argument.

During the moot counsel should listen to the submissions of the opposing team carefully to work out what they are arguing. Counsel should check to make sure the opponent's arguments line up against his own. If responding, counsel cannot respond to a point not appealed by the appellants. This means if the appellants chose to argue a side issue, responding counsel must adapt their argument to counter the side issue. It is important to do thorough research so counsel is aware of the side issues that could come up. Also counsel should be aware of how the opposition argue their submissions so counsel will know how to structure his rebuttals. If junior counsel has presented his argument then he should listen and pass information to help his senior. Teamwork between counsel should be made clear for the judge.

Once all counsel have made their arguments the judge will take a moment to gather his thoughts before passing judgment on the law and then the moot. As moots are often competitive it is important for counsel to shake hands and thank all participants for their contributions. Good team spirit and manners are as important after the moot as they are during it.

Summary

11.3 This chapter has:

1. addressed the final preparations for the moot competition;
2. provided guidance on the dress code required;
3. provided guidance on what counsel should take to the moot;
4. addressed the procedure for the moot including the entrance of the judge; and
5. provided guidance on what counsel should do before and after presenting counsel's argument.

Chapter 12

ADVICE FOR THE JUDGE

Introduction

This chapter aims to provide the judge with guidance on procedural **12.1**
points of a moot including what to take into account when marking
competitors' arguments. This chapter advises how to receive and check
authority; how much time to allow competitors and what to do when
a competitor runs out of time; how to deal with interruptions; what
approach to take when questioning counsel; and what approach to take
when giving judgment.

Receiving Authority

The judge must check to see that counsel gives a full citation including the **12.2**
name of the judge being cited and whether the judgment is assenting or
dissenting with the majority. If counsel fails to give relevant information
then the judge should ask for the missing information, including a full
citation. This can make an interesting question and often catches counsel
off guard if they do not know the case well enough. If counsel does not
know whether the judgment is assenting or dissenting or whose judgment
it is then this is evidence to suggest incomplete preparation and should be
taken into account when marking.

The Facts of the Case

In a moot, if case law is cited as authority, then counsel citing the authority **12.3**
must offer the facts of the case. It is at the discretion of the judge whether
or not to request the facts and often there will be no requirement to hear
them. However, if counsel demonstrates a lack of knowledge of the facts
then it suggests that counsel does not have a sound understanding of the
case. Failure by counsel to offer a summary of the facts of the case being
cited should be taken into account when marking.

Timing

12.4   The judge must decide if counsel should be allowed extra time. It is generally accepted that once time has lapsed counsel will be allowed to finished counsel's current point of law and conclude. However, citing new authority or beginning a new argument after time has lapsed is generally not accepted. The purpose of a moot is to teach counsel to make a concise argument. Allowing unlimited time to make an argument would remove the need for counsel to make decisions about how to structure an argument and what to present to the judge.

The judge should note the time that counsel has taken as recorded by the clerk. It is unfair for one team to be restricted to twenty-five minutes while the other team is allowed to stretch their argument over thirty-five minutes. Structuring a concise argument is a vital skill. The judge must take account of this when marking.

Interruptions

12.5   Although rarely occurring, interruption by counsel for the opposition side is not allowed while one counsel is speaking. If this does occur, the judge should deal with this swiftly. The judge may grant counsel of the same side permission to converse briefly. However, no extra time is given for this. Should the moot competition be interrupted by an unforeseen circumstance, the judge retains the power to allow a competitor additional time to compensate for the interruption.

Questioning Counsel

12.6   The purpose of questioning counsel should be to establish the strength of their argument and not merely the depth of their understanding of the law. The judge should ask each counsel roughly the same number of questions. If counsel cannot answer a question a judge should encourage counsel to move on and prevent counsel too much discomfort or delay in the moot, but would take the inability to answer into account when assessing the mooting performance. The judge is encouraged to ask questions at any time to seek clarification on a point of law being made.

Judgment

12.7   The judge will not get the opportunity to retire to make a decision on his judgment. This is different from a real court procedure. However, the judge may take a few minutes to gather his thoughts before giving a judgment, sometimes retiring from the moot room to consider the arguments. Judgment given on the law should be reasoned, short and should link in with the arguments counsel have presented. Judgment on the winners of the moot should be given after judgment on the law. Feedback can be given to the competitors during the judgment or thereafter. When giving feedback, it is useful if the judge gives brief examples of problems of understanding, strategy or style and suggests how the competitors can improve.

Summary

This chapter has provided the judge with guidance on: **12.8**

1. procedural points of a moot including what to take into account when marking;
2. how to receive and check authority;
3. how much time to allow competitors when time has elapsed;
4. how to deal with interruptions;
5. what approach to take when questioning counsel; and
6. what approach to take when giving the judgment on the law and the moot.

Chapter 13

ADVICE FOR THE CLERK

Introduction

The clerk plays a central but background role in mooting competitions. It **13.1** is important that both competitors and the judge are aware of the role of the clerk. This chapter outlines the role of the clerk as chief administrator of the moot. The clerk may not always be the host or the organiser of the moot, however, the clerk is integral to the smooth running of the moot as the clerk is the only person who can advise the judge on procedure during the mooting competition.

The Role of the Clerk

The central role of the clerk is chief administrator of the moot. Aside **13.2** from this the clerk has three principal responsibilities. These three responsibilities are: assisting the judge; managing the authorities at the moot; and timing each competitor's argument.

Assisting the Judge

The clerk should bring water, pens and paper to the moot in case the judge **13.3** or any counsel needs them. The clerk must meet with the judge briefly before the moot begins. At this time, the judge may ask the clerk anything about the rules of the moot such as timing or order of arguments. The judge may request the clerk's advice on mooting procedures at any time during the moot. When the moot is about to begin, the clerk must take the judge outside the room. The clerk must then enter the room, call the court to order and lead in the judge. The judge may at any time during the moot consult the clerk on an issue of procedure or with any concern or problem.

Management of Authorities

The clerk will use the two lists of authorities given by the competitors **13.4** on the day before the moot. The clerk must check that the authorities have been correctly cited and note which citations are common to both teams. If an authority has been incorrectly cited or cannot be found the clerk must contact the relevant team and attempt to locate the intended authority. It is the responsibility of the clerk to gather the authorities from the law library, liaise with librarians about their removal and transport the authorities to the location of the moot.

When a case is cited to the judge it is the clerk's responsibility to find the relevant book and page. Counsel should stop talking while this is being done. The clerk must then pass the open text to the judge. It is the judge's responsibility to find the paragraph, line and word. Thus, it is advisable for the clerk to bookmark the relevant pages before the moot begins.

Counsel can provide a folder with photocopied versions of the relevant cited authority in plastic pockets to the clerk. The folder must be presented to the clerk before the moot begins and it is the clerk's responsibility to check through the folder to ensure the material is legitimate and correctly copied. Bookmarking the relevant pages in the folder along with numbering the plastic pockets or dividers, attaching sticky labels to the top of the page, highlighting and underlining of the photocopied authority are all possible. However, any form of annotation on the photocopied authority is not permitted. Written submissions and other material not on the list of authorities provided the day before the moot are not normally permitted, unless the rules of the moot specifically allow this.

It is at the discretion of the clerk whether to accept a folder of authority. If a folder is accepted, the clerk need only pass the folder to the judge at the beginning of the relevant counsel's argument. From that time it will become counsel's responsibility to direct the judge to the relevant case and page within the folder.

Timing

13.5 The clerk is responsible for time monitoring. The clerk must begin timing when a counsel first addresses the judge at the lectern and stop timing when that counsel concludes his argument. The clerk must inform the judge of the time each counsel has taken during their argument including any extra time allowed.

When counsel has two minutes left the clerk must hold up a sign bearing the writing '2 minutes' until it is clear the current counsel has seen the sign and is aware of the time remaining. When counsel has one minute remaining the clerk must hold up a sign bearing the writing '1 minute' until that counsel is aware. When counsel has reached his maximum time allowed the clerk must hold up a sign bearing the writing 'TIME' until that counsel is aware. The clerk must not stop timing counsel until the counsel has concluded his argument. This is to ensure appropriate marking for time management.

Summary

This chapter has: **13.6**

1. established the importance of the clerk in a moot competition;
2. outlined the role of the clerk;
3. addressed the role of the clerk in assisting the judge;
4. addressed the role of the clerk in managing the authorities of a moot competition; and
5. addressed the role of the clerk in timing each competitor.

Chapter 14

MOOTING COMPETITIONS

Introduction

This chapter is dedicated to listing the types of mooting competitions open **14.1** to students from Scottish law schools and providing contact information for participation in competitions. This chapter deals with internal Scottish university mooting competitions and Scottish national mooting competitions. This chapter also outlines some of the popular English national competitions and deals with popular international mooting competitions. The purpose of this chapter is to point competitors in the right direction for taking part in competitions.

Internal Scottish University Mooting Competitions

There are many internal mooting competitions at Scottish universities. **14.2** Most Scottish universities offering the Degree of Bachelor of Laws (LLB) or other qualifying professional degree programmes run mooting competitions which are either organised by individual staff members or by mooting societies of students undertaking the degree programme. For example, the University of Aberdeen offers a first-year mooting competition specifically for first-year LLB students and the university also offers the 'Faculty competition' which allows all years of the LLB programme at the University of Aberdeen to compete. The University of Glasgow's mooting society operates the Dean's Cup Competition. Details of internal mooting competitions at each individual university can be found by contacting the university's law school. Contact details of each university's law school offering a LLB programme in Scotland at the time of writing are listed below in figure 5.[21]

---

[21] Universities offering the LLB program sourced from UCAS <www.ucas.ac.uk>. Law school contact details sourced from respective law school's websites.

Figure 5   Law School Contact Details

The University of Aberdeen
School of Law
University of Aberdeen
Taylor Building
Aberdeen
AB24 3UB
Scotland
Tel: 01224 272441
Fax: 01224 272442
www.abdn.ac.uk/law

The University of Edinburgh
School of Law
University of Edinburgh
Old College
South Bridge
Edinburgh
EH8 9YL
Scotland
Email: law@ed.ac.uk
Tel: 0131 650 2008
Fax: 0131 650 6317
www.law.ed.ac.uk

University of Abertay Dundee
Dundee Business School
University of Abertay Dundee
Bell Street
Dundee
DD1 1HG
Scotland
Tel: 01382 308401
Fax: 01382 308877
www.abertay.ac.uk

Edinburgh Napier University
Edinburgh Napier University
Craiglockhart Campus
Edinburgh
EH14 1DJ
Scotland
Email: info@napier.ac.uk
Tel: 08452 606040
Fax: 01314 556464
www.napier.ac.uk

Glasgow Caledonian University
School of Law and Social Sciences
Glasgow Caledonian University
Cowcaddens Road
Glasgow
G4 0BA
Scotland
Email: lss@gcal.ac.uk
Tel: 01413 318429
Fax: 01413 313798
www.gcal.ac.uk/lss/divisions/
divisionoflaw

University of Dundee
School of Law
University of Dundee
Dundee
DD1 4HN
Scotland
Tel: 01382 384461
www.dundee.ac.uk/law

The Robert Gordon University
Aberdeen Business School
The Robert Gordon University
Garthdee Road
Aberdeen
AB10 7QE
Scotland
Tel: 01224 262000
Fax: 01224 263838
www.rgu.ac.uk/

University of Glasgow
5–9 Stair Building
The Square
University of Glasgow
Glasgow
G12 8QQ
Scotland
Email: enquiries@law.gla.ac.uk
Tel: 01413 303583
Fax: 01413 304900
www.gla.ac.uk/departments/
schooloflaw

The University of Strathclyde	The University of Stirling
The Law School	*School of Law*
Level 3	*Airthrey Castle*
The Lord Hope Building	*University of Stirling*
St James' Road	*Stirling*
Glasgow	*FK9 4LA*
G4 0LT	*Scotland*
Scotland	Email: law@stir.ac.uk
Tel: 01415 483738	Tel: 01786 467282
www.law.strath.ac.uk	Fax: 01786 467353
	www.law.stir.ac.uk

Scottish National Mooting Competitions

There are three main national or inter-university mooting competitions **14.3**
in Scotland. The Alexander Stone Scottish Intervarsity Moot Court
competition, organised by the University of Glasgow, is available to all
law students undertaking an LLB in Scots law at a Scottish university. The
Granite City Moot Court Competition is an annual competition between
students from the University of Aberdeen and Robert Gordon University
and is organised by the University of Aberdeen. The Sheriff Moot is an
annual competition between LLB students from Glasgow Law School and
Strathclyde Law School and is organised and hosted by Glasgow Sheriff
Court. These competitions provide the opportunity for law students
to practice the vital skills gained in mooting. Competitions are often
sponsored by prestigious law firms and judged by respected sheriffs and
Lords Ordinary.

Alexander Stone Scottish Intervarsity Moot Court Competition **14.3.1**

Run by:	The University of Glasgow
Open to:	All students undertaking an LLB in Scots law
Website:	www.gla.ac.uk/departments/schooloflaw
Address:	5–9 Stair Building
	The Square
	University of Glasgow
	Glasgow
	G12 8QQ
	Scotland
Email:	enquiries@law.gla.ac.uk
Telephone:	01413 303583
Fax:	01413 304900

14.3.2 *Granite City (Aberdeen v Robert Gordon) University Moot Court Competition*

Run by:	The University of Aberdeen
Open to:	LLB Students at the University of Aberdeen and Robert Gordon University
Website:	www.abdn.ac.uk/law
Address:	School of Law
	University of Aberdeen
	Taylor Building
	Aberdeen
	AB24 3UB
	Scotland
Email:	law433@abdn.ac.uk
Telephone:	01224 272441
Fax:	01224 272442

14.3.3 *Sheriff Moot*

Run by:	Glasgow Sheriff Court
Open to:	LLB Students at Glasgow Law School or Strathclyde Law School
Website:	www.scotcourts.gov.uk
Address:	Sheriff Court of Glasgow
	PO Box 23
	1 Carlton Place
	Glasgow
	G5 9DA
Email:	glasgow@scotcourts.gov.uk
Telephone:	0141 429 8888
Fax:	0141 4185248

English National Mooting Competitions

14.4 Although organised in England and often based on English law it is not uncommon for students undertaking a Scottish law degree to partake in English mooting competitions. There is much to benefit from practising law across the border in another legal system. The vital skills of research, analysis and presentation of an oral argument can be tested and advanced by taking part in competitions based on law that it is likely counsel will at first be entirely unfamiliar with. Below is a short list of some of the more popular English mooting competitions. Some of these competitions are open not only to law students within the United Kingdom but also to law students from foreign law schools, making the competition more dynamic and exciting.

The English-Speaking Union Essex Court Chambers National Mooting Competition   **14.4.1**

Run by:	The English-Speaking Union
Sponsors:	Essex Court Chambers
Website:	http://www.essexcourt.net/mooting/page.asp?p=134
Address:	The English-Speaking Union
	Dartmouth House
	37 Charles Street
	London
	W1J 5ED
	UK
Email:	Rosie_unwin@esu.org
Telephone:	020 7529 1550
Fax:	020 7495 6108

Oxford University Press and BPP National Mooting Competition   **14.4.2**

Run by:	Oxford University Press and BPP Law School
Sponsors:	N/A
Website:	http://www.oup.co.uk/oxfordtextbooks/law/mooting/
Address:	c/o OUP Mooting Competition,
	Higher Education Department
	Oxford University Press
	Great Clarendon Street
	Oxford
	OX2 6DP
Email:	mooting.uk@oup.com
Telephone:	01865 353273
Fax:	N/A

The Weekly Law Reports Mooting Competition   **14.4.3**

Run by:	Incorporated Council of Law Reporting
Sponsors:	Justis and the Law Society
Website:	http://www.lawreports.co.uk/Mooting/MootHome.htm
Address:	The Weekly Law Reports Mooting Competition
	Megarry House

	119 Chancery Lane
	London
	WC2A 1PP
Email:	mooting@iclr.co.uk
Telephone:	020 7242 6471
Fax:	020 7831 5247

14.4.4 *London University Mooting Shield*

Run by:	London University Mooting Shield
Sponsors:	Allen & Overy
	Three Verulam Buildings
	Field Court Chambers
	5 Stone Buildings
Website:	http://www.lumshield.co.uk/
Address:	London Universities Mooting Shield,
	Bentham House
	Endsleigh Gardens
	London
	WC1H OEG
Email:	dan.jackson@lumshield.co.uk
Telephone:	N/A
Fax:	N/A

14.4.5 *English Law Students Association Moot Court Competition*

Run by:	English Law Students Association
Sponsors:	N/A
Website:	http://www.elsalondon.org/
Address:	ELSA London
	The Law School
	King's College
	London
	WC2R 2LS
Email:	president@elsalondon.org
Telephone:	N/A
Fax:	N/A

14.4.6 *Inner Temple Inter Varsity Mooting Competition*

Run by:	Inner Temple Mooting Society
Sponsors:	The Inner Temple
Website:	http://www.itmoot.org/

Address:	N/A
Email:	innertemplemooting@gmail.com
Telephone:	N/A
Fax:	N/A

UK Environmental Law Association Mooting Competition **14.4.7**

Run by:	UK Environmental Law Association
Sponsors:	N/A
Website:	http://www.ukela.org/
Address:	2 Harcourt Buildings
	Temple
	London
	EC4Y 9DB
Email:	clerks@twoharcourtbldgs.demon.co.uk
Telephone:	020 7353 8415
Fax:	020 7353 7622

International Competitions

As well as taking part in English national competitions it would also be **14.5** of benefit to law students undertaking a LLB at a Scottish university to take part in international mooting competitions. Universities and legal establishments throughout the world recognise the advantage of allowing law students to experience researching and arguing law that is foreign to their own jurisdiction. The opportunity to research international law and law of individual jurisdictions is a new experience for many law students and expands on the important research and analysis skills that all good law students have mastered. There are more international competitions than it would be appropriate to list in this short section, so only a few of the popular international competitions are listed below.

Commonwealth Mooting Competition **14.5.1**

Run by:	Queensland University of Technology
Sponsors:	N/A
Website:	www.law.qut.edu.au/about/moots/comps/common/index
Address:	2 George Street
	GPO Box 2434
	Brisbane QLD 4001
	Australia

Email:	r.macdonald@qut.edu.au
Telephone:	0061 738641100
Fax:	0061 7 38642121

14.5.2 *European Law Moot Court*

Run by:	The European Law Moot Court Society
Sponsors:	Mannheimer Swartling, Garrigues, Norton Rose
Website:	zealot.mrnet.pt/mootcourt/
Address:	European Law Moot Court Competition
	Organizing Team
	Faculdade de Direito de Lisboa
	Apartado 52103
	1700 Lisboa
	Portugal
Email:	ot@mail.fd.ul.pt
Telephone:	351 21 793 46 24
Fax:	351 21 796 60 37

14.5.3 *European Law Students' Association (EMC2) Moot Court Competition*

Run by:	The European Law Students' Association
Sponsors:	The World Trade Institute, Magisters
Website:	www.elsamootcourt.org
Address:	The European Law Students' Association – ELSA
	International
	239 Bd General Jacques 1050
	Brussels
	Belgium
Email:	elsa@brutele.be
Telephone:	32 2 646 26 26
Fax:	32 2 646 29 23

14.5.4 *Philip C. Jessup International Law Moot Court Competition*

Run by:	International Law Students Association
Sponsors:	N/A
Website:	www.ilsa.org/jessup
Address:	25 East Jackson Boulevard
	Suite 518
	Chicago

Illinois 60604
United States of America

Email:	ilsa@ilsa.org
Telephone:	(001) 202 299 9101
Fax:	(001) 202 299 9102

Telders International Law Moot Court Competition 14.5.5

Run by:	Leiden University
Sponsors:	N/A
Website:	www.grotiuscentre.org/com/doc.asp?DocID=346
Address:	P.O. Box 13228
	2501 EE The Hague
	The Netherlands
Email:	grotiuscentre@campusdenhaag.nl
Telephone:	0031 70 310 8606
Fax:	0031 70 310 8609

Summary

This chapter has: **14.6**

1. addressed Internal Scottish University Mooting competitions;
2. dealt with Scottish National Mooting competitions;
3. outlined popular English national competitions; and
4. introduced international competitions.

Chapter 15

CONCLUSION

The communication skills and logical reasoning which underpin legal argument will always remain the same. However, like all professional skills, the art of legal argument will continue to develop and evolve to meet the demands of the legal industry and wider society.

Taking part in mooting competitions at university will provide law students with valuable skills that can be easily transferred into the working environment of the legal profession and other aspects of life. The ability to analyse a problem and make a concise, reasoned response is a useful life-long skill that students and postgraduates of law schools throughout Scotland will never stop learning.

Appendix 1 below uses a real moot problem to provide a full example of how to make a structured and reasoned logical argument using the two stage method. The two stage method is a basic method of constructing a legal argument. Having analysed this method it is appropriate to build on the two stage method by combing it with real experience and further study on legal argument.

The further reading section below will give law students some guidance on where to turn for more information on the skill of legal argument. However, it will be of particular benefit for law students to visit the High Court of Justiciary, Court of Session or Sheriff Courts to see how advocates and solicitors make legal argument in a real court room setting.

FURTHER READING

1. C Kee, *The Art of Argument: A Guide to Mooting* (Cambridge University Press, New York, 2006).

2. D Pope and D Hill, *Mooting and Advocacy Skills* (Sweet & Maxwell, London, 2007).

3. J Snape and G Watt, *The Cavendish Guide to Mooting* (Cavendish Publishing Limited, London, 1997).

4. K Ashley, *Modeling Legal Argument: Reasoning with Cases and Hypotheticals* (Massachusetts Institute of Technology Press, United States of America, 1990).

5. M Anderson with E Miller, *A Guide to Mooting Aberdeen University Law Mooting Society* (2nd edn, Oswalds, Edinburgh, 1993).

6. P Dobson and B Fitzpatrick, *The Observer Book of Moots* (Sweet & Maxwell, London, 1986).

7. T Kaye and L Townley, *Blackstone's Book of Moots* (Blackstone Press Limited, London, 1996).

8. W A Wilson, *Introductory Essays on Scots Law* (2nd edn, W Green & Son, Edinburgh, 1984).

MOOTING EXAMPLE: CRIMINAL LAW

Introduction: The Two Stage Mooting Method

In this example the moot problem is based on criminal law and deals with **A1.1** the common law crime of breach of the peace. This example will follow the argument made by junior counsel for the appellant as counsel follows the two stage method outlined in Chapters 3 and 4.

This example is perfect for the first-time competitor as it ties in with the LLB core topic of criminal law. In order to keep this example simple it avoids dealing with complex law on the crime of breach of the peace but instead concentrates on the method of making the legal argument and presenting it to the court. For this reason, not much law is cited and most of the analysis revolves around applying the basic legal test to the facts of the particular case.

In figure 6 below, the role of junior counsel for the appellant is reiterated from Chapter 2 and references are given to the relevant sections in Chapter 4. Below in figure 7 is the moot problem 'Smith against Her Majesties Advocate'.

Figure 6   The Role of Junior Counsel for the Appellant

Junior counsel for the appellant (see Chapter 2)	References
Introduces himself to the judge	para 4.2
Offers to the judge a brief outline of the facts of the case at first instance	para 4.3
Puts the appellant's questions to the court	para 4.4
Outlines the submissions to be discussed by the appellants, indicating which of these will be dealt with by each counsel	para 4.5
Provides the structure of his argument / deals with his submissions	para 4.6
Concludes his submissions and argument	para 4.7

Figure 7 *The Moot Problem:* Smith v HM Advocate

Smith v HM Advocate

Mr Andrew Gray Smith attended his cousin's 25th birthday party at 216 Rosemount Place, Aberdeen on a sunny, Saturday afternoon. The festivities lasted many hours and at around 11pm Mr Smith, along with many companions, progressed into the city centre to take advantage of the colourful night life of Aberdeen.

In the early hours of Sunday morning, PC Johnston was called to a crowded Belmont Street where Mr Smith was found leaning up against a local shop window swearing at security door staff who had not allowed him access to make use of the facilities at the popular public house 'The Lamb's Head'. PC Johnston attempted to arrest Mr Smith on the basis of his shouting and swearing in public and his general disorder. Mr Smith, in his intoxicated state, believed he was being abducted and called out for aid to passers-by whilst swearing repeatedly at PC Johnston. In the several minutes of struggle that followed, Mr Smith caught the eye of some attractive ladies out on a hen night. He called out to them making rather inappropriate and highly explicit sexual requests. The group of ladies appeared undisturbed and stumbled on shouting in a drunken stupor, typical of members of the public at that hour on Belmont Street.

Mr Smith was charged on summary complaint in Aberdeen Sheriff Court that; '(1) at 2.35am on the 15th of June 2009, at Belmont Street in Aberdeen city centre, you did conduct yourself in a disorderly manner, shout and swear in the presence of local security staff, a group of ladies, police officers and commit a breach of the peace; (2) at 2.40am on the 15th of June 2009, at Belmont Street in Aberdeen city centre, you did conduct yourself in a disorderly manner, brawl with the police and commit a breach of the peace.

At Aberdeen Sheriff Court, Sheriff John, having heard the evidence, found the crime to be proved beyond reasonable doubt, considering the behaviour to be more than just a simple nuisance or irritation to members of the public. Sheriff John held that the definition of breach of the peace was settled, as established in the leading case of *Smith v Donnelly* 2001 SLT 1007. At paragraph 17 of the court's opinion, as delivered by Lord Coulsfield, it is stated *'What is required to constitute the crime is conduct severe enough to cause alarm to ordinary people and threaten serious disturbance to the community'.* On application of this legal test the Sheriff John found Mr Smith guilty as charged.

As it was Mr Smith's first offence Sheriff John required him to pay a £200 fine. The court granted leave for appeal.

The case will appear before the High Court in Edinburgh consisting of a bench of seven judges.

You are acting as Mr Smith's counsel appealing against the decision by Sheriff John at first instance.

Stage 1: The Problem and Moot Point

Before junior counsel can prepare his argument counsel must first research the problem and the law. In this section, junior counsel will work through stage 1 'The problem and moot point' as addressed in Chapter 3. Below in figure 8 is a reminder of figure 2 from Chapter 3 which shows the first approach to the moot problem. **A2.1**

Figure 8   Stage 1: The problem and Moot Point

Stage 1: The problem and moot point Chapter 3	Reference
Read the problem and Identify the Field	para 3.2
Research	para 3.3
Identify the central moot points	para 3.4
Allocation of points of law	para 3.5

Read the problem and identify the relevant field of law

As with all counsel, junior counsel for the appellant must identify the relevant field of law and research it prior to establishing the moot points. After reading the problem it will be apparent to counsel that the field of law is Scots criminal law and the relevant area of law is the crime 'breach of the peace'. Junior counsel will have confirmed that he is acting as junior counsel for Mr Smith who is the appellant in this matter. This means that junior counsel for the appellant will be arguing that the sheriff should not have found Mr Smith guilty of breach of the peace. Junior counsel for the appellant will also notice that the points of law for appeal are not given **A2.2** and he will have to extract the grounds of appeal himself. Junior counsel will have a short discussion with his senior counsel to ensure they are both aware of the field of law and what side they are arguing. They may also have discussion on the research that will be done, suggesting books or important cases to read. Junior counsel would then begin background research on the field of law.

Research

A2.3 The case *Smith v Donnelly*[22] is mentioned in the problem and is the first port of call for background reading. Junior counsel would also read cases cited in *Smith v Donnelly*. Background reading in Gordon, *The Criminal Law of Scotland*[23] would give some insight into the crime of breach of the peace and further reading. *Stair's Institutions*[24] and *Bell's Commentaries*[25] may also provide a general feel for the history of the crime. It may also be beneficial for junior counsel for the appellant to refer to his course and lecture notes on the crime breach of the peace and to student texts on Scots criminal law. These texts will give the most up-to-date depiction of the crime of breach of the peace. Junior counsel should read Jones and Christie.[26]

Having read these texts junior counsel would have a reasonable background knowledge of the crime of breach of the peace and its history. This background knowledge would include the facts that:

(a) Breach of the peace is a common law crime; as such there is no statutory authority on it.

(b) Breach of the peace as a crime has derived from the crimes of mobbing and rioting.

Junior counsel for the appellant will have also discovered many cases that contain potentially relevant legal principles. Only a few are listed below for illustration.

Authority	Potential[27] principle
(a) *Smith v Donnelly* 2001 SCCR 800	Outlines the legal test for breach of the peace. Swearing does not amount to a

---

[22] *Smith v Donnelly* 2001 SLT 1007.
[23] Gordon, *The Criminal Law of Scotland* (3rd edn, 2005).
[24] Stair, *Institutions of the Law of Scotland*.
[25] Bell, *Commentaries on the Law of Scotland*.
[26] T H Jones and M G A Christie, *Criminal Law* (4th edn, 2008).
[27] Early in counsel's research, junior counsel will not have established the exact principles of each case.

		breach of the peace. Refusal to co-operate with the police does not amount to a breach of the peace.
(b)	*Harris v HMA* 2009 SLT 1078	There must be a 'public element' to the crime.
(c)	*Paterson v HMA* 2008 SLT 465	A small group of individuals in a private house is sufficient to constitute a 'public element'. There must be the potential for both alarm to ordinary people and the threat of serious disturbance to the community.
(d)	*Jones v Carnegie* 2004 SCCR 361	Applies *Smith v Donnelly* / outlines the test.
(e)	*Dyer v Hutchinson* 2006 SCCR 377	No evidence of alarm is needed. The test applies in the context of the situation
(f)	*Donaldson v Vannet* 1998 SCCR 422	The test for breach of the peace is objective.
(g)	*Raffaelli v Heatly* 1949 JC 101	Conduct that is merely annoyance is insufficient.
(h)	*Derrett v Lockhart* 1991 SCCR 109	Fighting in public amounts to a breach of the peace.
(i)	*Dyer v Brady* 2006 SCCR 629	Each case must be decided on its own merits.
(j)	*Hughes v Crowe* 1993 SCCR 320	Mens rea is to be inferred from the nature and quality of the acts.
(k)	*Kinnaird v Higson* 2001 SCCR 427	Swearing does not amount to a breach of the peace.
(l)	*McDonald v Heywood* 2002 SCCR 92	Refusal to cooperate with the police does not amount to a breach of the peace
(m)	*MacDougall v Dochree* 1992 JC 154	Deliberately committing a breach of the peace to prevent criminal activities might be a defence.

Having established basic background knowledge of the field of law and a reasonable understanding of the moot problem junior counsel for the appellant would then begin identifying the central moot points. These will circle around the potential arguments available.

Identify the central moot points

Junior counsel for the appellant must dismiss side issues and work out the central moot points. This is the analytical stage of a moot and it is where

A2.4

excellent counsels will excel in finding the moot point. This process of analysis is done by reading the problem and comparing it with the research carried out. Having reread the problem and analysed it in comparison with the research just completed, junior counsel for the appellant will note that there are two charges and as such counsel for the appellant must argue two central points:

Central moot points

(a) The first central issue is: did Mr Smith's conduct amount to a breach of the peace following relevant legal authority when he shouted and swore at door staff? (Research suggests that shouting and swearing are not a breach of the peace *Smith v Donnelly, Kinnaird v Higson.*)

(b) The second central issue is: did Mr Smith's conduct amount to a breach of the peace when he refused to cooperate with the police? (Research suggests that refusal to cooperate with the police does not amount to a breach of the peace *McDonald v Heywood, Smith v Donnelly.*)

Side issues

(a) The issue that Mr Smith was trying to prevent his kidnapping and acting in self-defence when he called out may be of relevance as a legal issue. Only through further research will it be possible to confirm the weight of this issue.

(b) The issue that Mr Smith was intoxicated is irrelevant as no defence can be grounded on it.

(c) The defence of attempting to prevent criminal activities while deliberately causing a breach of the peace (as established in *MacDougall v Dochree*) would be unsuccessful as Mr Smith was not in fact being abducted, thus he could not claim that his breach of the peace was to prevent a crime.

Allocation of points of law

A2.5   Once junior counsel for the appellant has identified the central moot points counsel should discuss with senior counsel for the appellant which moot points each counsel should argue. In this case junior counsel for the appellant would argue the point:

(a) *Number 1:* The first charge is irrelevant since the act of shouting and swearing in the context of the situation did not amount to conduct severe enough to cause alarm to ordinary people and threaten serious disturbance to the community and as such does not amount to a breach of the peace under Scots law

Junior counsel would leave the more complicated submission Number 2 to his senior to argue.

(b) *Number 2:* The second charge is irrelevant since the act of refusing to co-operate with the police is insufficent to amount to the actus reus of breach of the peace and thus fails to amount to a breach of the peace in Scots law.

Once counsel has established the moot points then it is time for counsel to make an argument.

Stage 2: Making the Legal Argument: Chapter 4

Now that junior counsel for the appellant has researched the problem and the field of law it is time for junior counsel to start making an argument. Chapter 4 deals with stage 2 'making a legal argument'. Junior counsel for the appellant will now follow stage 2 in order to make his legal argument. **A3.1**

It will be useful to bear in mind the responsibilities that junior counsel for the appellant has while approaching stage 2. Refer back to the role of junior counsel at figure 5 above to see what structure counsel will be following when making the argument.

Figure 9   Stage 2: Making the Argument

Stage 2: Making the Argument Chapter 4	Reference
Introduction	para 4.2
Outlining the facts	para 4.3
Putting a question to the court	para 4.4
Submissions	para 4.5
Stating the structure of the argument /addressing the submission	para 4.6
Forming a concrete conclusion	para 4.7

Junior counsel's introduction

A3.2 Junior counsel should begin by introducing himself and stating who he represents.

> *'Good evening My Lord. If it pleases Your Lordship my name is Steven Mair and I am junior counsel for the appellant Mr Smith.'*

Outline the facts / offer to the judge a brief outline of the facts of the case at first instance[28]

A3.3 Junior counsel for the appellant will then offer the judge the facts of the case at first instance.

> *'Before I begin, does Your Lordship require a brief synopsis of the case at first instance?'*

If the judge states not, then counsel will move to stating his submissions:

> *'If it pleases Your Lordship I will now outline the points of law to be discussed by the appellants.'*

If the judge states, 'Yes' then counsel must provide a synopsis of the case:

> *'My Lord, the findings in fact of the case before us are as follows: Mr Andrew Gray Smith attended his cousin's 25th birthday party at 216 Rosemount Place Aberdeen on Saturday afternoon. At 11pm Mr Smith progressed into Aberdeen city centre to take advantage of the Aberdeen's night life. In the early hours of Sunday morning PC Johnston was called to Belmont Street where Mr Smith was leaning up against a shop window while swearing at security door staff who had not allowed him entry to The Lamb's Head to use their facilities. PC Johnstone attempted to arrest Mr Smith on the basis of his shouting and swearing in public and his general disorder. Mr Smith, in his intoxicated state, believed PC Johnstone was attempting to abduct him. Mr Smith called out for aid and swore repeatedly at PC Johnstone. During the struggle Mr Smith called out to a group of attractive ladies on a hen night. Mr Smith made rather inappropriate and highly explicit sexual requests. The group of ladies appeared undisturbed and stumbled on shouting in a drunken stupor, typical of members of the public at that hour on Belmont Street.'*

---

[28] Remember from para 8.5 that junior counsel must offer the judge the facts of the case at first instance as well as highlighting important facts.

'Mr Smith was charged on summary complaint in Aberdeen Sheriff Court that:

"(1) at 2.35am on the 15th of June 2009, at Belmont Street in Aberdeen city centre, you did conduct yourself in a disorderly manner, shout and swear in the presence of local security door staff, a group of ladies, police officers and commit a breach of the peace;

(2) at 2.40am on the 15th of June 2009, at Belmont Street in Aberdeen city centre, you did conduct yourself in a disorderly manner, brawl with the police and commit a breach of the peace;

At Aberdeen Sheriff Court at first instance Sheriff John considered, beyond reasonable doubt, the behaviour to be more than just a simple nuisance or irritation to members of the public. Sheriff John held that the definition of breach of the peace was settled, as established in the leading case of Smith against Donnelly two-thousand-and-one Scots Law Times at page one-thousand-and-seven. At paragraph 17 of the court's opinion, as delivered by Lord Coulsfield, it is stated, 'What is required to constitute the crime is conduct severe enough to cause alarm to ordinary people and threaten serious disturbance to the community". On application of this legal test Sheriff John found Mr Smith guilty as charged. Thank you My Lord.'

Puts the question to the court

This question will be the question that counsel seeks to answer in his **A3.4** submissions. In this case, junior counsel wants to show that his client is not guilty of the crime of breach of the peace by stating that his actions do not fall within the scope of the crime.

'My Lord, the question before the court this evening is: Did Mr Smith's actions in the early hours of the 15th of June 2009 fall within the legal test for breach of the peace as established in Smith v Donnelly that, conduct has to be severe enough to cause alarm to ordinary people and threaten serious disturbance to the community.'

Submissions / outlines the submissions to be discussed by the appellants, indicating which of these will be dealt with by each counsel

Junior counsel seeks to outline the answers that counsel will give **A3.5** to the question put to the court. In this case, junior counsel is stating that his clients actions do not fall within the scope of the crime of breach of the peace and thus his client should have been acquitted.

'My Lord I would like to begin with the submissions of the appellants.'

'Number 1: The first charge is irrelevant since the act of shouting and swearing in the context of the situation did not amount to conduct severe enough to cause alarm to ordinary people and threaten serious disturbance to the community and as such does not amount to a breach of the peace under Scots law.'

'Number 2: The second charge is irrelevant since the act of refusing to cooperate with the police is insufficient to amount to the actus reaus of breach of the peace and thus fails to amount to a breach of the peace in Scots law.'

'The first submission, My Lord will be dealt with by myself. My learned senior will deal with the second submission. Thank you My Lord that concludes the points of law to be discussed by the appellants. If it pleases Your Lordship I would now like to turn to my first submission.'

Structure the argument / Addressing the submission

A3.6 Junior counsel will then seek to answer the question put to the court using logical legal argument to convince the judge that his answer is the correct answer to follow. Junior counsel first reminds the judge of the outline of his answer and then provides the full structure of his answer before dealing with the bulk of his logical legal argument.

'I am obliged My Lord. My Lord, my first submission is that: the first charge is irrelevant since the act of shouting and swearing in the context of the situation did not amount to conduct severe enough to cause alarm to ordinary people and threaten serious disturbance to the community and as such does not amount to a breach of the peace under Scots law.'

'In order to support this submission I intend to analyse the established test for breach of the peace. I then intend to apply that test to the facts of the case before the court today. An analysis of the facts of the case will reveal that there is no direct evidence of alarm being caused. With this in mind I will then establish what is needed for the court to objectively infer that alarm was caused. Having established this requirement I will then analyse the findings in fact of the case to show that the court is unable to draw an inference that Mr Smith's conduct is severe enough to cause alarm to ordinary people and threaten serious disturbance to the community.'

'The established test for breach of the peace as outlined in the moot problem from the case of Smith against Donnelly is as follows: "What is *required to constitute the crime is conduct severe enough to cause alarm to ordinary people and threaten serious disturbance to the community".'*

'An analysis of this test reveals that there must be conduct which is alarming and disturbing to any ordinary person and the conduct must threaten serious disturbance to the community. The question thus put to the court, My Lord, is; "Was Mr Smith's conduct alarming and disturbing to any ordinary person and did Mr Smith's conduct threaten serious disturbance to the community? An analysis of the facts is in order."'

'If Your Lordship would care to turn his attention to the moot problem page headed Smith *against* Her Majesty's Advocate. *I am reading from paragraph two where it states:*

"In the early hours of Sunday morning PC Johnston was called to a crowded Belmont Street where Mr Smith was found leaning up against a local shop window swearing at security door staff who had not allowed him access to make use of the facilities at the popular public house 'The Lamb's Head'. PC Johnstone attempted to arrest Mr Smith on the basis of his shouting and swearing in public and his general disorder. Mr Smith, in his intoxicated state, believed he was being abducted and called out for aid to passers-by whilst swearing repeatedly at PC Johnston. In the several minutes of struggle that followed Mr Smith caught the eye of some attractive ladies out on a hen night. He called out to them making rather inappropriate and highly explicit sexual requests. The group of ladies appeared undisturbed and stumbled on shouting in a drunken stupor typical of members of the public at that hour on Belmont street."

'My Lord, at no place in the findings in fact of the case at first instance does it state that an individual is suffering alarm or annoyance. Neither does it state in the facts at first instance that there was a threat to serious disturbance to the community. For this reason in order for a charge of breach of the peace to be successful the court must objectively infer that the conduct was alarming and disturbing to any ordinary person and threatened serious disturbance to the community.'

'I now wish to turn to the case of Smith *against* Donnelly *which provides the requirements for the court to make an inference. If Your Lordship would turn his attention to the case of* Pamela Smith *against* Christopher C. Donnelly, *reported in the two-thousand-and-one Scottish Criminal Case Reports, at page eight-hundred-and-six. I am reading from the opinion of the court as delivered by Lord Coulsfield, paragraph fifteen, the fifth paragraph down, the quoted section opposite the letter E, beginning "It follows therefore." Does Your Lordship have the relevant passage?'*

If the judge does, then proceed, if the judge does not then counsel should repeat the citation and ensure that the judge does have the correct passage.

> 'It is worth noting that the facts of the case are not materially tied to the point of law decided. However I am prepared to provide Your Lordship with a brief synopsis of the case if necessary.'

If the judge does request the facts then junior counsel should provide a short outline of the facts only a few sentences in length at most.

> 'In this passage the court is endorsing the dictum of Lord Justice-General Clyde at page seventy in the opinion of the court in the case of Young against Heatly. The Lord Justice-General Clyde had stated: "It follows therefore that it is not essential for the constitution of this crime that witnesses should be produced who speak to being alarmed or annoyed. At the same time, however, I consider that a very special case requires to be made out by the prosecution if a conviction for breach of the peace is to follow in the absence of such evidence of alarm or annoyance. For then the nature of the conduct giving rise to the offence must be so flagrant as to entitle the court to draw the necessary inference from the conduct itself".'

> 'It is clear from Lord Justice-General Clyde's remarks in the case of Young against Heatly as endorsed in the case of Smith against Donnelly that in order for a court to draw the necessary inference that, in the context of the situation the conduct was alarming and disturbing to any ordinary person and that there was a threat of serious disturbance to the community, the nature of the conduct must be flagrant.'

> 'I submit to Your Lordship that in this case the nature of the behaviour was not obvious enough for the court to draw the necessary inference. The context of the situation was the busy, colourful, alcohol-fuelled night life of Aberdeen's city centre. The shouting and swearing was carried out to battle hardened security door staff and drink-stupefied women who were unable to find the conduct as genuinely alarming and disturbing in the circumstances. Had the context of the situation been different then the court would have been entitled to draw the necessary inferences. For example had the shouting and swearing been carried out in Aberdeen City Library then in that context the conduct would be so flagrant as to allow the court to draw the necessary inferences that the conduct would have been genuinely alarming and disturbing to any ordinary person and that the conduct may have amounted to a threat of serious disturbance to the community.'

Forming a concrete conclusion / concludes his submissions and argument

Having produced a logical legal argument and correctly structured an **A3.7**
answer to the question put to the court counsel then forms a strong
conclusion reminding the judge of his answer to the question put to the
court.

> *'In conclusion My Lord for this reason I submit to Your Lordship that the
> first charge is irrelevant since the act of shouting and swearing on Belmont
> Street at 2.40am did not amount to conduct severe enough to cause alarm
> to ordinary people and threaten serious disturbance to the community and
> as such does not amount to a breach of the peace under Scots law. In
> conclusion I submit to Your Lordship that appeal should be upheld.'*
>
> *'That, My Lord, concludes the arguments I wish to submit on behalf
> of the appellant, unless there are any issues on which I may be of further
> assistance?'*

If the judge has questions to ask then counsel should answer them. When
the judge indicates that he has finished with counsel then counsel should
thank the judge for hearing his argument and give a small bow to the
judge when leaving the lectern.

> *'I am obliged, My lord.'*

INDEX OF EXAMPLES

INDEX OF FIGURES

INDEX